"Walter Brueggemann ...ful and compelling interpreter of the Bible as it bears on current social and religious crises. Here he discerns how the arrogant American exceptionalism of 'God's new Israel' has been powerfully informed by the biblical ideology of God's chosen people and the exceptionalism of the ancient Jerusalem elite. . . . *Reality, Grief, Hope* is timely, prophetic, and very well done."

— **RICHARD HORSLEY**
University of Massachusetts, Boston

"Brueggemann's connection of Israelite royal ideology with U.S. exceptionalism is provocative and courageous. His interweaving of modern poetry and political theory with Scripture texts powerfully amplifies the countercultural exhortation of the ancient prophets: covenantal faith must be lived in mutual relationship with the poor. Brueggemann calls communities gathered around Scripture to be catalytic in their dismantling of structures of social privilege, economic exploitation, and racism. This is a compelling and urgently needed book."

— **CAROLYN J. SHARP**
Yale Divinity School

"Challenges the churches to a prophetic task in the face of the twin ills in American exceptionalism: complacency when things go well and self-centered despair when (as after 9/11) they go badly. Brueggemann shows how the witness of the Old Testament prophets can be a resource for faithful hope that does not rest on cynical self-concern. Calling for a wider vision of society and its possible futures than the imperialistic self-assertion of an elite, this book calls for inclusion and for justice."

— **JOHN BARTON**
Oriel College, Oxford

REALITY, GRIEF, HOPE

Three Urgent Prophetic Tasks

WALTER BRUEGGEMANN

Foreword by

Louis Stulman

WILLIAM B. EERDMANS PUBLISHING COMPANY

GRAND RAPIDS, MICHIGAN / CAMBRIDGE, U.K.

Published 2014 by
Wm. B. Eerdmans Publishing Co.
2140 Oak Industrial Drive N.E., Grand Rapids, Michigan 49505 /
P.O. Box 163, Cambridge CB3 9PU U.K.
www.eerdmans.com

Printed in the United States of America

19 18 17 16 15 14   7 6 5 4 3

Library of Congress Cataloging-in-Publication Data

Brueggemann, Walter.
Reality, grief, hope : three urgent prophetic tasks / Walter Brueggemann;
foreword by Louis Stulman.
pages   cm
Includes bibliographical references.
ISBN 978-0-8028-7072-8 (pbk.: alk. paper)
1. Prophecy — Religious aspects — Christianity. 2. Hope — Religious aspects —
Christianity. 3. Bible. Isaiah — Criticism, interpretation, etc. 4. Bible. Jeremiah —
Criticism, interpretation, etc. 5. Bible. Lamentations — Criticism,
interpretation, etc. 6. Laments in the Bible.   I. Title.

BR115.P8B78   2014

234'.25 — dc23

2013038807

Scripture quotations are from the *New Revised Standard Version of the Bible* © 1989 by the Division of Christian Education, National Council of the Churches of Christ in the United States of America, used by permission.

Excerpts from the poems "Thanksgiving Day in the U.S." and "Hope" are from *Threatened with Resurrection: Prayers and Poems from an Exile Guatemalan*, by Julia Esquivel, copyright © 1982, 1994 Brethren Press, Elgin, Illinois. Used with permission.

Excerpt from "Tortures" from POEMS NEW AND COLLECTED 1957-1997 by Wislawa Szymborksa, translated from the Polish by Stanislaw Baranczak and Clare Cavanagh. English translation copyright © 1998 by Houghton Mifflin Harcourt Publishing Company. Reprinted by permission of Houghton Mifflin Harcourt Publishing Company. All rights reserved.

To the Memory

of

J. Davison Philips

Contents

Foreword

It is great pleasure to write this foreword for Walter Brueggemann's new book, *Reality, Grief, Hope: Three Urgent Prophetic Tasks*. Walter is a dear friend and an esteemed colleague. Indeed, he has been a formative presence in my life for many years.

My first encounter with his work came in the late 1970s. In a graduate school seminar led by Herbert B. Huffmon, I read three of Walter's earliest works, *Tradition for Crisis: A Study in Hosea* (John Knox, 1968), *The Vitality of the Old Testament Traditions* (with Hans Walter Wolff; John Knox, 1975), and the recently published *The Prophetic Imagination* (Fortress, 1978). These books made an enormous impression on me. In the first place, they were beautifully written and theologically penetrating. I was also captivated by their audacity to move beyond the historical perimeters of the text to the contemporary world. Reviewers recognized this quality as well. One, for instance, noted that *Tradition for Crisis* "relates the prophets to contemporary Christians," and another recognized the convincing lines of argumentation "for a contemporary view of Hosea." It was apparent from the start that Brueggemann's close reading of the biblical text was neither neutral nor dispassionate, as the rubrics of the field demanded. Rather, his nuanced exposition was attentive to ecclesial realities — especially those related to pastoral ministry — and the larger society. Put differently, Brueggemann's earliest writings already reflected a firm commitment to "make the interface of ancient text and contemporary community . . . poignant and palpable."[1]

In my first decade of teaching at a small theological school in Ohio, I deployed Walter's works in almost all of my classes. On the Pentateuch we read his commentary on Genesis (John Knox, 1982). In my Prophets class I assigned *The Prophetic Imagination* (Fortress, 1978) along with the equally eloquent *Hopeful Imagination* (Fortress, 1986). Required reading in Psalms and Wisdom Literature included *In Man We Trust* (John Knox, 1972) and *The Message of the Psalms* (Augsburg, 1984). Brueggemann was a good companion in those classes which, I gladly concede, were essentially teach-taught (I suspect many others could make a similar confession). It never surprised me that his robust engagement with the text and rich interpretive move into contemporaneity resonated with my students and became their model for exegetical and homiletic practice. They had little interest in reading Scripture as an archive of the past, and even less enthusiasm for bracketing out theological questions. Brueggemann's dogged commitment to weave contemporary issues into his interpretive work was a godsend to us.

In the 1990s I had the privilege of working with Walter as well as with Kathleen O'Connor, Pete Diamond, Ronald Clements, and Robert Carroll in a Society of Biblical Literature Group on the book of Jeremiah. Kathleen, Pete, and I were relatively new to the enterprise, perhaps with a few fresh ideas, but clearly standing on the shoulders of giants. What developed from those conversations on Jeremiah was a decisive shift from preoccupations with compositional history and the biography of the prophet to a text-centered and reader-centered exploration mindful of synchronicity, theological engagement, hermeneutics, and contem-

---

1. Walter Brueggemann, *An Introduction to the Old Testament: The Canon and Christian Imagination* (Louisville: Westminster John Knox, 2003), xi.

poraneity. Brueggemann punctuated the project with a reference to George Steiner's definition of critic and reader: "The critic prescribes a syllabus; the reader is answerable to and internalizes a canon."[2] Once again he was determined to engage in interpretive perspectives that were generative, evocative, and germane to the church and society — or in his own words, "to move through the paces of criticism so that this unreadable script [of Jeremiah] may rescript our unreadable lived reality."[3]

Since then Walter has written hundreds of articles and books, including Old Testament theologies, numerous commentaries, introductions to the Old Testament, and collections of sermons and prayers.[4] This remarkable body of work is diverse and wide-ranging; in many respects it is as undomesticated as the holy text it explicates. If there is a *Mitte*, a core, or quality that holds together Brueggemann's diverse and dynamic oeuvre, however, I wonder if it is not a propensity for reading the biblical text as "a living countertestimony" and a stirring witness to "the unsettled God" whose words ever disrupt our predictable categories and habits of injustice. In more prosaic terms, Walter's intense theological engagement with the Bible never ignores the pressing issues that confound the church, pastoral ministry, and society. No wonder this leading and generative voice in the church is also one of our most daring cultural critics.

All this is a rather circuitous way of saying that this book is vintage Brueggemann! It is theologically rich, passionately said, deeply disturbing, and timely. As we have come to expect, Brueg-

2. See Walter Brueggemann, "Next Steps in Jeremiah Studies?" in *Troubling Jeremiah*, ed. A. R. Pete Diamond, Kathleen M. O'Connor, and Louis Stulman (Journal for the Study of the Old Testament Supplement 260; Sheffield: Sheffield Academic, 1999), 404-22 (421).

3. Brueggemann, "Next Steps in Jeremiah Studies?" 422.

4. For an exhaustive bibliography, see Walter Brueggemann with Carolyn J. Sharp, *Living Countertestimony: Conversations with Walter Brueggemann* (Louisville: Westminster John Knox, 2012), 165-99.

gemann brings a remarkable clarity to the project. His point of
departure is the destruction of Jerusalem in 587 b.c.e. and the
cluster of texts that engage in a contested communal dialogue
over the meaning of the disaster. He explores the significance
of the catastrophe for a Jerusalem establishment that had long
enjoyed a life of privilege and entitlement. Of particular interest
is the prophetic response to this alliance and its governing ideol-
ogy/theology of exceptionalism. And Brueggemann brings to the
foreground the lingering sense of loss and the praxis of grief — a
practice that is an antidote to denial, indeed a practice that leaves
a deep scar on the text and our lives.

Brueggemann's move into contemporaneity is telling and urgent — perhaps "urgent," as the title suggests, is the operative
word. One can discern in these pages a palpable sense of urgency
out of which a clarion call for action emerges. Here Brueggemann
as cultural exegete confronts the dominant forces of our time —
market ideology, monologic politics, enlightenment rationality,
globalization, and military arrangements, to name only a few.
I will not provide too many spoilers at this point other than to
say that this book turns dangerous. (Per Pirkeby, "The point at
which Art is found is the point where what is intriguing turns
dangerous.") It names names, takes on principalities and powers
that vie for our souls, and lays bare realities that "vex both church
and society." Brueggemann dares to expose the ideological arrangements that sustain our lives of privilege, albeit at great cost.

Brueggemann's incisive critique is no less impressive than his
call to action, action that targets the many tentacles of U.S. exceptionalism — "the distorted view of societal reality sustained by
the ideology that breeds unrealistic notions of entitlement, privilege, and superiority" (see below, p. 33). This prophetic posture
requires the trenchant work of truth-telling and denial-breaking,
as well as the practice of grief. It also demands the enactment of
an alternative defined by "an *alliance of God and neighbor* against

such acquisitive exploitation, so that there is no possibility of loving God without loving neighbor" (p. 36). Brueggemann brings these complex workings into greater focus in an exposé on two intermingled metanarratives, the totalizing narrative of empire and the particularizing narrative of the neighborhood. Here he parses two conflicting readings of reality which find expression in competing social constructions. Much is at stake, for the church and its ministry, along with our culture, in reading these narratives with clarity and courage.

Not long ago NPR host Krista Tippett described Walter Brueggemann as "a kind of theological rock star." Such language might put off some readers and might even embarrass Walter, but I find it instructive. Even in the academy and the church we honor our sages and celebrate our poets whose words sustain us and haunt us back to life.

Several years ago my wife Kate and I spent a night at Asbury Park, New Jersey, before a Bruce Springsteen concert. While at breakfast we met a woman who had just arrived from Brussels for her *eighteenth* Springsteen concert, fifteen of which had been in the States. As newbies, not groupies, we asked her why she had spent so much time and money on these concerts, and without missing a beat she told us, "Bruce gets it, he gets me, and puts it all into words."

As this good book bears out, Walter Brueggemann "gets it." He gets the church, he gets the culture, and he has put it into words for over four decades — words that linger and enliven, that disturb and unsettle, words on which many of us have long come to depend.

LOUIS STULMAN

Acknowledgements

I am especially grateful to my friend and colleague Louis Stulman, who has read this manuscript carefully, has encouraged me to proceed with it, and has written a most generous foreword. He and I have a long history of thinking together about the prophets. I am delighted to dedicate this book to the memory of J. Davison Philips, long-time president of Columbia Theological Seminary. It was he who appointed me to the faculty of the seminary where I have enjoyed long years of happy collegiality. I was privileged to witness the magnetic power of Dr. Philips, together with his honesty, his courage, his wisdom, and his good humor. He followed in the tradition of the prophets, and I am glad to express my abiding appreciation for him.

WALTER BRUEGGEMANN
Columbia Theological Seminary
Epiphany, 2013

I

Three Urgent Prophetic Tasks: An Introduction

There is no doubt that the destruction of Jerusalem in 587 B.C.E. is the defining historical event in the literature of the Old Testament. That destruction and the dislocation that followed amounted to a huge upheaval of every dimension of Israel's life, including displacement of theological certitude. I propose that one can trace that theological crisis according to:

- confidence in the ideology of chosenness held by the Jerusalem establishment,
- denial amid the crisis that that ideology had failed and was not sustainable, and
- despair when the denial was broken and reality was faced.

In what follows, I will propose, acknowledging the cultural divide, that the crisis of 9/11 amounted to this same kind of defining dislocation in our society as did the destruction of Jerusalem in that ancient society. The impact of 9/11, along with the loss of life, was an important turn in societal ideology. We have been forced to face new waves of vulnerability that we had not before acknowledged. The force of that fresh awareness is evident in the various scrambles for security that have ensued since that event. I propose that in our society, as in that ancient society, one can trace our theological crisis according to

- confidence in the ideology of exceptionalism,
- denial, amid the crisis, that that ideology has failed and is not sustainable, and
- despair once the denial is broken and reality is faced.

In the ancient world of Israel, the prophetic corpus of the Old Testament amounts to a massive and relatively coherent response to the crisis, albeit expressed in a variety of images. Thus I propose that the prophetic response to the crisis of the destruction of Jerusalem consists in

- the assertion of critical reality in the face of an ideology of chosenness,
- voiced grief in the face of denial, and
- buoyant hope as a counter to despair.

In what follows I will propose that current "prophetic ministry" has an opportunity to engage in the same three tasks as did those ancient prophets:

- the articulation of reality that is too often disguised by our ideology of exceptionalism,
- the performance of grief about loss in response to the denial that the ideology of exceptionalism is unsustainable, and
- articulation of hope in response to despair that variously produces moralism, hedonism, and violence.

Thus in each of the chapters that follows I will pursue

- an articulation of an ancient conventional conviction,
- an articulation of a contemporary uncritical claim,
- an articulation of prophetic response to an ancient conventional practice, and

- a suggestion of a contemporary prophetic response to a contemporary uncritical assumption.

To the extent that my analysis is persuasive, to that extent the church, in its prophetic practice, has important work to do; that work, I suggest, is indispensable for the future viability of our society. It is, moreover, work that is likely to remain undone until it is undertaken by a faithful, courageous, emancipated church.

II

Reality amid Ideology

Pretend you're happy when you're blue
It isn't very hard to do
And you'll find happiness without an end
Whenever you pretend.

BRENDA LEE

The destruction of Jerusalem in 587 B.C.E. at the hands of the Babylonians constituted the defining experience of ancient Israel given us in the Old Testament. This was "a supreme social and, therefore, religious catastrophe."[1] That destruction shattered the socio-political life of the community and destroyed the social institutions that ordered that society. More important, that destruction reached into the depth of Israel's theological understanding and called into question the most elemental theological certitudes that Israel had imagined. What follows here is a reflection upon that crisis and the engagement made with it by the prophets, in anticipation and in response to it.

I will propose in what follows, moreover, that in our contemporary social crisis in the United States, the destruction of the

---

1. Norman K. Gottwald, *Studies in the Book of Lamentations* (Studies in Biblical Theology 14; Chicago: Allenson, 1954), 64.

World Trade Center and the intended destruction of the Pentagon on 9/11 together constituted a quite parallel experience in this country. On that day the attacks not only caused many deaths, but disrupted the economic life of our society. More than that, I propose, the attacks reached to the depth of theological self-understanding in the United States as a nation and called into question the most elemental theological certitudes that we have been able to imagine. Thus the symbolic import of that attack is more elemental and more urgent than the visible, physical-political concreteness. It is for that reason that the event continues to draw our attention and our pathos. In what follows I will consider the engagement of contemporary prophetic voices with that event, both in anticipation and in response to it.

I.

Royal Jerusalem in ancient Israel was deeply enthralled to an ideology of chosenness. The Jerusalem destroyed in 587 B.C.E. was a product and carrier of the elemental conviction of Israel — and more specifically of the urban elite in the Jerusalem establishment — that it was indeed YHWH's chosen people and so enjoyed the full commitment of YHWH as patron and guarantor. That conviction of chosenness had old rootage in the traditions of Israel, however one assesses the historicity of that tradition. Michael Walzer has most recently reviewed the double rootage of chosenness and covenant in the tradition. On the one hand, the covenant YHWH made with Abraham is a "covenant of the flesh" having to do with the family ("seed") of Abraham.[2] It is often noted that this covenant is based on the unconditional

---

2. Michael Walzer, *In God's Shadow: Politics in the Hebrew Bible* (New Haven: Yale University Press, 2012), 1-2.

promise of God to Abraham, an unconditionality that was later important to the Jerusalem establishment. On the other hand, the covenant made at Sinai was made with "a mixed multitude," not an identifiable family group, and is a "covenant of law."[3] As is often noted of the Sinai covenant, it is conditional, based on the defining "if" of covenantal obedience (Exodus 19:5). Walzer terms the first of these a "birth model" of covenant that favors "nativism and exclusion."[4] The second he terms the "adherence model" that offers "a politics of openness and welcome, proselytism and expansion." This covenant can be entered into by the consent of those who had not previously joined, by agreeing to the terms and conditions of the covenant. Such adherence is evident, for example, in the negotiations of Joshua 24. The two covenants together constitute the basis of Israel's theological self-understanding.

That covenantal self-understanding, moreover, was dramatically encoded in the covenantal rhetoric of Deuteronomy, a tradition surely formulated in the middle years of the Davidic dynasty:

For you are a people holy to the LORD your God; the LORD your God has chosen you out of all the peoples on earth to be his people, his treasured possession. (Deuteronomy 7:6)

For you are a people holy to the LORD your God; it is you the LORD has chosen out of all the peoples on earth to be his people, his treasured possession. (Deuteronomy 14:2)

The horizon of Deuteronomy is largely committed to the "covenant of law":

---

3. Walzer, *In God's Shadow*, 2. Walzer translates the "rabble" (*ᵃsapsup*) as "riff-raff," a nice homeopoetic reading.

4. Walzer, *In God's Shadow*, 3.

Today you have obtained the LORD's agreement: to be your God; and for you to walk in his ways, to keep his statutes, his commandments, and his ordinances, and to obey him. Today the LORD has obtained your agreement: to be his treasured people, as he promised you, and to keep his commandments; for him to set you high above all nations that he has made, in praise and in fame and in honor; and for you to be a people holy to the LORD your God, as he promised. (Deuteronomy 26:17-19)

An effort is made in the tradition to connect the covenant of Sinai to the promises to Abraham, thus coalescing the tradition with a coherent claim (see Deuteronomy 6:10; 9:5, 27; 29:13; 30:20). In this consolidation of the notion of chosenness, it was not necessary, so it seems, to sort out the distinctions between the two traditions. In its various nuances, the tradition consistently attested the peculiar status of Israel as YHWH's chosen people.

These traditions, as we have them and without regard to what they may have been in their origin, have now been filtered through the forceful claims of the Jerusalem establishment. It is impossible to overstate the power of the Jerusalem establishment in galvanizing and making normative the conviction of being chosen for covenant. Thus I suggest that the use made of these old claims by the Jerusalem establishment amounts to the articulation of an ideology that would frame the life, faith, and imagination of the community and would consequently shape policy. I use the term "ideology," slippery as it is, to indicate the defining importance of the memory of chosenness for the Jerusalem establishment in giving legitimacy to its power and its way in the world. As is well known, Karl Marx took "ideology" to refer to "false consciousness," a misconstrual of reality to serve particular interests.[5] Paul

---

5. The insight of Marx has been advanced by Michel Foucault, who has seen most clearly how "power and truth" travel together.

Ricoeur, more benignly, has understood "ideology" to refer to any framing story of a society, without reference to its legitimacy or distorting function.[6] I intend here to use the term in the way that Marx understood it, so that the old traditions of chosenness are utilized to legitimate the socio-economic, political, liturgic claims of the Jerusalem establishment. I suggest that Solomon's transport of the ark of the covenant into the city and into his temple is a dramatic indication of the way in which the old tradition has been co-opted for pragmatic use in Jerusalem (see 1 Kings 8:1-13). The ark is the icon of the old covenantal tradition vouching for the presence of YHWH; but that icon has now been preempted by the Jerusalem establishment as an emblem of its legitimacy. What are legitimated in that act are the power, privilege, and entitlement of the urban elite who clustered around the king and who lived off the produce of the peasant economy that surrounded the city. The enumeration of the tax districts of Solomon (1 Kings 4:7-19) and the inventory of consumption in Solomon's entourage (1 Kings 4:22-23) evidence that the urban establishment lived very well off of that peasant produce.

In the development of the tradition, however, that socioeconomic advantage is effectively disguised in the tradition that came to function in liturgical settings. I suggest that the following texts evidence the "ideological cover-up" that intentionally hid the social-economic reality that only belatedly and negatively erupted among the peasants.[7]

Psalm 78 is a long recital of the history of Israel with YHWH. The Psalm juxtaposes YHWH's unfailing generosity toward Israel and Israel's insistent recalcitrance. Israel

6. Paul Ricoeur, *Lectures on Ideology and Utopia*, ed. George H. Taylor (New York: Columbia University Press, 1986).

7. The peasant eruption against the urban elites is narrated in 1 Kings 12:1-19.

refused to walk according to his law (v. 10)
had no faith in God (v. 22)
did not believe in his wonders (v. 32)
were not true to his covenant. (v. 37)

Eventually,

they provoked him to anger with their high places;
    they moved him to jealousy with their idols.
When God heard, he was full of wrath,
    and he utterly rejected Israel.
He abandoned his dwelling at Shiloh,
    the tent where he dwelt among mortals. (vv. 58-60)

The abandonment of Shiloh is crucial, for Shiloh was the old shrine that apparently was the seat of authority in the old covenantal tradition (see 1 Samuel 1:3; Jeremiah 7:12-14). As the Psalm reaches its conclusion, it traces the movement of YHWH from the abandonment of Shiloh to the double choice of Jerusalem and David:

He rejected the tent of Joseph,
    he did not choose the tribe of Ephraim;
but *he chose* the tribe of Judah,
    Mount Zion, which he loves. . . .
He chose his servant David,
    and took him from the sheepfolds; . . .
to be the shepherd of his people Jacob,
    of Israel, his inheritance. (vv. 67-71)

The culmination of the history of Israel is the divine choice of David and Mount Zion, king and temple!

That conviction of chosenness is detailed in the narrative tra-

9

dition of Israel. The choosing of David (and his dynasty) is told in the long narrative that begins with David's anointing (1 Samuel 16) and culminates in his anointing as "king over Israel" (2 Samuel 5:3). That narrative is consolidated in the report of 2 Samuel 7, wherein David is granted, via Nathan, an assurance of divine fidelity for all time:

> When he commits iniquity, I will punish him with a rod such as mortals use, with blows inflicted by human beings. But I will not take my steadfast love from him, as I took it from Saul, whom I put away from before you. Your house and your kingdom shall be made sure forever before me; your throne shall be established forever. (vv. 14-16)

None of the vagaries of history can disrupt this divine commitment. Thus David and his entourage, the entire company of urban elites, are given guarantees that do not require engagement with the facts on the ground.

The choosing of Judah and Mount Zion eventuates in the temple of Solomon, the great urban icon of divine presence and guarantee. The great dedication of the temple of Solomon in 1 Kings 8 constitutes an act of liturgic legitimation when the ark is brought into the temple. That liturgic act, surely conducted and articulated by priests on the royal payroll, includes the entire power structure of society. It ends with the arrival of the ark with a "cloud" that is reminiscent of the arrival of the divine glory in the tabernacle of Exodus 40:34-38 (1 Kings 8:1-11). That arrival of divine glory evoked a choral anthem that confirmed Jerusalem as the abiding residence of YHWH:

> The LORD has said that he would dwell in thick darkness.
> I have built you an exalted house,
>   a place for you to dwell in forever. (vv. 12-13)

The distinction in the narrative between the "inner sanctuary" (holy of holies) and the "holy place" indicates a liturgical hierarchy of order and privilege that matches the hierarchal economy of the urban scene (see v. 6). Thus YHWH is now shrouded in thick darkness to which only designated royal priests have access, the ones who function as mediators of the divine presence to the more common public. The liturgic decision of YHWH to dwell in that most holy place is forever, in Hebrew expressed in the plural "forever and ever," not to be disrupted or disturbed by any historical intervention. The intent of the liturgy is to put the residence of YHWH (and so the claims of the urban establishment) beyond the reach of historical contingency.

The convergence of the royal promise and the temple residence amounts to a liturgic legitimation whereby the old chosenness of Israel has now been concretized and specified in the Jerusalem regime. The enhancement of that centralized and legitimated authority is advanced by the "Songs of Zion" that celebrate the wonder of the temple. These songs sing of the wonder and beauty of the temple and the city that will "contain" YHWH. Thus in Psalm 76:

> In Judah God is known,
>   his name is great in Israel.
> His abode has been established in Salem,
>   his dwelling place in Zion. (vv. 1-2)

The God who dwells there is awesome indeed as the creator and arbiter of the claims of the oppressed:

> But you are indeed awesome! . . .
> From the heavens you uttered judgment;
>   the earth feared and was still

> when God rose up to establish judgment,
>> to save all the oppressed of the earth. (vv. 7-9)

As Ben Ollenburger has argued, a claim of the temple is that the God resident there is committed to justice for the poor and the oppressed.[8] It is, moreover, the same God

> who cuts off the spirit of princes,
>> who inspires fear in the kings of the earth. (v. 12)

In Psalm 84, familiar from Brahms, the temple is a safe, happy place for all creatures. The extent to which the temple is committed in its liturgical practice to the monarchy is in dispute, and Ollenburger is at pain to distinguish between the two. But in verse 9, surely the king is in view:

> Behold our shield, O God;
>> look on the face of your anointed.

Thus we may recognize that the king is the sponsor and patron of the temple, its chief practitioner, and for that reason the one who "hosts" God's presence. The king is tied into a palpable divine presence. As God is patron of Jerusalem, so David is patron of the temple in which God resides.

The best known of the Songs of Zion is Psalm 46, which affirms God's resolve to keep the city safe. In the environs of social power, the acutely felt crisis is never guilt. It is rather chaos and disorder. That chaos and disorder is reflected, for example, in the royal Psalm 2, wherein the kings of the earth threaten the order and

---

8. Ben C. Ollenburger, *Zion, the City of the Great King: A Theological Symbol of the Jerusalem Cult* (Journal for the Study of the Old Testament Supplement 41; Sheffield: Sheffield Academic, 1987).

rule of YHWH. In that Psalm it is "his anointed" who is designated to defeat the threat of the nations:

> I will tell of the decree of the LORD:
> He said to me, "You are my son;
>   today I have begotten you.
> Ask of me, and I will make the nations your heritage,
>   and the ends of the earth your possession.
> You shall break them with a rod of iron,
>   and dash them in pieces like a potter's vessel." (vv. 7-9)

The nations are called to serve the anointed of YHWH:

> Now therefore, O kings, be wise;
>   be warned, O rulers of the earth.
> Serve the LORD with fear,
>   with trembling kiss his feet,
> or he will be angry, and you will perish in the way;
>   for his wrath is quickly kindled. (vv. 10-11)

In Psalm 46, the threat of chaos is of a different order from that of the nations in Psalm 2:

> Therefore we will not fear,
>   though the earth should change,
>   though the mountains shake in the heart of the sea;
> though its waters roar and foam,
>   though the mountains tremble with its tumult. (vv. 2-3)

But the Psalm does not finally distinguish between cosmic chaos, characterized in verses 2-3, and political chaos in verse 6:

> The nations are in an uproar, the kingdoms totter;
>   he utters his voice, the earth melts.

In both cases concerning cosmic chaos and political chaos, the same Hebrew term *moṭ* is used, rendered in one usage as "shake," in the other as "totter"! In both cases, the order designed by YHWH, cosmic and political, is under assault. The faithful, however, are not fearful or dismayed. They are convinced and here reassured that the order of YHWH, defended by the king in Psalm 2 and assured by the temple, will prevail. The "with us" in the repeated formula of verses 7, 11, "The LORD of hosts is with us," bespeaks a temple presence; but it is a temple presence with the resolve and means to maintain order.

It is clear that the Jerusalem establishment appeals to the old covenantal tradition chosenness. When that tradition is drawn close to the urban reality of Jerusalem with its economic advantage and its political domination of the peasant economy round about, it is clear that the claims of dynasty and temple have come to serve as legitimation for a socio-economic, political power arrangement. It is precisely that legitimation that insists that the present power arrangement not only had divine approval, but was guaranteed to perpetuity.

That guarantee is voiced in lavish articulation in the royal Psalm 89 in which the Davidic dynasty is linked to divine fidelity that cannot be disrupted or disturbed. The Psalm is permeated with the language of "steadfast love and faithfulness," a word pair that became a tag-word for divine commitment to the city, its practices, and its institutions (vv. 1-2, 14, 24). The connection is made, moreover, to creation, so that the Jerusalem establishment came to have cosmic significance and is a component of the created order:

> But I will not remove from him my steadfast love,
>   or be false to my faithfulness.
> I will not violate my covenant,
>   or alter the word that went forth from my lips.

Once and for all I have sworn by my holiness;
    I will not lie to David.
His line shall continue forever,
    and his throne endure before me like the sun.
It shall be established forever like the moon,
    an enduring witness in the skies. (Psalm 89:33-37)

We can for now leave open the question whether this "ideology" is simply a framing narrative (with Ricoeur) or whether it is a sustained act of "false consciousness" (Marx). Obviously the framers and practitioners of it do not tell us. When one moves to prophetic engagement, it becomes clear that these sustained practices of legitimation are indeed acts of false consciousness that had narcoticized its adherents to the realities of life in the world around them. Those who trusted these reassuring claims did not notice and eventually did not care. They did not need to, because their most elemental liturgical recitals told them otherwise.

II.

The vocation of the prophets, in the face of such an enthralling ideology, is to penetrate and expose that ideology by appeal to the reality of the lived world, a reality that steadfastly refused to conform to the claims of that ideology. The prophetic tradition in the eighth and seventh centuries B.C.E. in ancient Israel runs parallel to the dynastic line of David. The prophets appear uncredentialed, without genealogy or impressive pedigree, each with a distinctive style and set of images. Given those important distinctions, they do nonetheless constitute something of a coherent testimony, and that is certainly what the tradition of the final form of the text means to suggest about them. It is credible to think that the prophets are not simply eruptive individual persons. They are, rather, situated in varying ways in an on-going interpretive tradition that is rooted in the old covenant of Sinai. As we have seen, however, that tradition has now been transposed into the ideology of urban Jerusalem to serve as legitimation for the power structure of the urban elites. In that context, these prophetic voices offer a perspective that has not been co-opted by or contained within the dominant ideology.

We cannot know how it is that they were able to resist such domestication, but they regularly attest to their outsider status with the formula "Thus saith the Lord." They claim to speak a word that is not derived from or informed by the dominant ideology. It will not surprise us that they claim to speak a word that refuses to accept the legitimacy of the dominant system that is broadly assumed in society. These voices, unwelcome as they were amid the dominant ideology, spoke a word of realism about the world, a realism that is grounded on the one hand in *the rule of YHWH* who had not been contained in the dominant ideology. They imagine a world in which YHWH is a lively character and an effective agent, the very claims that the royal-temple theology could not countenance. On the other hand, they are grounded in *the socio-economic reality of the peasant production system* that was in profound tension with the dominant system of consumption. The prophetic utterance characteristically reflects a subversive alliance of *the holy God* and *the peasant community,* both of whom fall outside the claim of that ideology. This alliance, is evident, for example, in the old Song of Deborah that celebrates the defeat of the "Canaanite kings," the early masters of the urban economy. The victory is celebrated in this mode:

Tell of it, you who ride on white donkeys,
    you who sit on rich carpets,
    and you who walk by the way.
To the sound of musicians at the watering places,

there they repeat the triumphs of the LORD,
  the triumphs of his peasantry in Israel. (Judges 5:10-11)

The last two lines in parallel remarkably attribute the victory both to YHWH and to the peasantry.

In the late text of Isaiah 57:15, the residence of God is attested in this way:

For thus says the high and lofty one
  who inhabits eternity, whose name is Holy:
I dwell in the high and lofty place,
  and also with those who are contrite and humble in spirit,
to revive the spirit of the humble,
  and to revive the heart to the contrite.

The dwelling of God is, on the one hand, in the heavenly place where the gods dwell; but remarkably, the divine dwelling is with the humble and lowly. Both claims fall outside the ideology of Jerusalem that gives little credit to the actuality of God and none at all to the peasants.

Thus I propose that prophetic utterance bears witness to reality that falls outside the purview of the ideology of Jerusalem. We have seen that that ideology specializes in "steadfast love and faithfulness," a word pair used to bespeak divine reliability for the status quo. I suggest that in the face of that usage, the best tag-word for prophetic utterance is the word pair "justice and righteousness," a word pair that concerns economic justice and neighborly solidarity. To be sure, the engine of ideology knew very well how to make use of such phrases. In celebrating Solomon, the narrative could report of him:

Because the LORD loved Israel forever, he has made you king
  to execute justice and righteousness. (1 Kings 10:9)

The use of the modifier "forever" makes clear that we are dealing with ideology that preempts the word pair for royal control. In such a context the word pair is blunted of critical poignancy. In Isaiah 9:7, moreover, the anticipation of the next great king (messiah) is that the coming king will rule well:

> He will establish and uphold it
> with justice and with righteousness
> from this time onward and forevermore.

Again the modifier "forevermore" is a bar against the reality of social contingency. The familiar royal titles in verse 6 bespeak an ideology that transcends the real-life world of social relationships. Most remarkably, in Psalm 89 which I have already considered, the poetry manages to bring together the two word pairs, one of which I have identified as a slogan for the dominant power arrangement and the other with force for prophetic alternative:

> *Righteousness and justice* are the foundation of your throne;
> *steadfast love and faithfulness* go before you. (Psalm 89:14)

Such a convergence of terms shows the way in which dominant ideology could preempt other claims and submit them to the needs and horizon of that urban enterprise.

But of course on the lips of the prophets, the phrase "justice and righteousness" takes on a sharpness that is very different from the accommodated use of the royal-priestly liturgy. The prophetic usage intends to penetrate the facade of the ideology and to expose it as a practice that is out of sync with covenantal requirements. The word pair recurs in the prophets with a harshness that is not to be accommodated:

Ah, you that turn justice to wormwood,
and bring righteousness to the ground.

(Amos 5:7; see 6:12)

And then positively:

But let justice roll down like waters,
and righteousness like an ever-flowing stream. (Amos 5:24)

In his Song of the Vineyard, Isaiah identifies the failure of Israel
as a failure to produce justice and righteousness:

He expected justice,
but saw bloodshed;
righteousness,
but heard a cry! (Isaiah 5:7)

Most poignantly, Jeremiah critiques King Jehoiakim with the
same words, only now he states them negatively:

Woe to him who builds his house by unrighteousness,
and his upper rooms by injustice. (Jeremiah 22:13)

The prophets expose the ideology-enthralled regime of Jerusalem as failing in covenantal, neighborly practice. In venturesome
poetry, they trace out the inescapable consequences of such a
neighborly default.

The prophets are voices of unrelenting realism in the face of
deceiving ideology. We may note two matters about their way of
speaking truth to power. First, there is a consistency of form in
their utterance that is called by interpreters a "speech of judgment," utterance that imagines a formal court filing against Israel.
That genre of speech includes both an indictment and a sentence.

The indictment is an opportunity to review all of the covenantal failures of the power structure. It will not surprise that the indictment basically concerns two matters, the abuse of neighbors, especially vulnerable neighbors, and the dishonoring of God. And of course those two go together as violation of the two commandments, love God and love neighbor. The urban elite, they assert, have not loved God. That refusal is evident in arrogance, pride, and self-indulgence, as they imagine they are the center of the universe and are not accountable to anyone for anything. The dominant culture has, in its chosenness, failed to love neighbor and so has failed to regard the weak, poor, and vulnerable as legitimate members of the community. The elite have manipulated the markets, paid low wages, foreclosed on homes, and managed the economy in their own interest to the detriment of others.

The other element of the "speech of judgment," the sentence, imagines the future that is being generated by such actions. Sometimes the prophets only say "woe to you," which means "big trouble coming," big trouble coming irresistibly (see Isaiah 5:8-23; Habakkuk 2:7-19). Sometimes they imagine the coming of an attack by a foreign invader who, they say, is dispatched by God against God's people. Jeremiah can have God say:

> I am going to bring upon you
>   a nation from far away,
>   O house of Israel, says the LORD.
> It is an enduring nation,
>   it is an ancient nation,
> a nation whose language you do not know,
>   nor can you understand what they say.
> Their quiver is like an open tomb;
>   all of them are mighty warriors.
> They shall eat up your harvest and your food;
>   they shall eat up your sons and your daughters;

they shall eat up your flocks and your herds;
    they shall eat up your vines and your fig trees;
they shall destroy with the sword
    your fortified cities in which you trust. (Jeremiah 5:15-17)

Sometimes they imagine the undoing of creation, as though they knew about global warming (see Jeremiah 4:23-26). Hosea can list the Ten Commandments and see that the consequence of violation is a drought that exhibits the dismantling of creation:

Swearing, lying, and murder,
    and stealing and adultery break out;
    bloodshed follows bloodshed.
Therefore the land mourns,
    and all who live in it languish;
together with the wild animals
    and the birds of the air,
    even the fish of the sea are perishing. (Hosea 4:2-3)

What strikes one about the utterance of indictment and sentence (that may be uttered in many variations) is that the connection between violation and consequence is unbreakable and intransigent.[9] That connection is guaranteed by YHWH as the creator and cannot be overcome by any amount of shrewd technology. The structure of creation will not yield to big power or big money or big knowledge.

The prophets in their realism attest to the ways in which *God is mocked* and *neighbor is demeaned* by political arrogance, economic manipulation, and religious obtuseness. But the second thing that

9. On "deeds and consequences," see Patrick D. Miller Jr., *Sin and Judgment in the Prophets: A Stylistic and Theological Analysis* (Society of Biblical Literature Monograph Series 27; Chico: Scholars, 1982). The argument is partly based on the essay of Klaus Koch cited there.

strikes one about the recurring prophetic utterance of "speeches of judgment" is that they are daring, playful poetry with all kinds of risky images that are designed not only to instruct those held by the ideology, but to shock, dismay, and perhaps to move them emotionally to get back in touch with reality. It may all be about "justice and righteousness," but Hosea can imagine Israel as a "silly dove" that flits about (Hosea 7:11), or as a pancake half baked (7:8), or with an invading army that feels like terrorism (5:8-9), or as adulterers as hot as a heated oven (7:4), or like an attack of a vulture (8:1), or like a wild ass wandering about (8:9), or as a stone sinking into the water (10:7). Or Jeremiah can portray his contemporaries as those who depend on broken cisterns (Jeremiah 2:13), or as a chosen vine with degenerate fruit (2:21), or as a camel in heat (2:23), or as a bride who forgets her jewelry (2:32), or as a prostitute waiting on a street corner (4:30), or as a desperate mother dying in labor (4:31), or as a lusting stallion (5:8), or as the only bird that does not know when to migrate (8:7), or as a poor people without a doctor (8:22), or as a pile of corpses (9:22). The list goes on and on in a torrent of images and metaphors. The poetry is not primarily confrontational. Rather, it is probing, and subversive, and risky, like turning a kaleidoscope so that you can see it in many different ways. Because if we see our lives in many ways, we may discover that the single way of chosenness is not a reliable certitude, but rather a distortion of reality.

Such reality is not given in cold statistics. It is given in shocking, relational imagery, making clear that lived life in the world is in fact complex, fluid, and filled with risk. The prophets call the urban establishment to recognize that social reality is *populated by neighbors* and *occupied by YHWH,* who is not a settled truth but rather a subversive agent who comes like a whirlwind or a lion or a winnowing fork. The neighbors among us wait to be treated like neighbors. The God who moves amid the poetic utterance will not be settled or domesticated or managed. Thus reality is always at risk. And how the powerful conduct themselves will determine the outcome. The acknowledgement of YHWH as the central agent will lead to well-being; but disregard of YHWH will lead to disaster and disorder. Respect for the neighbor will make for safety; but disregard of the neighbor will result in violence and dismay.

This rich imagery is offered in order to express the unutterable but intransigent connection between policy and practice, on the one hand, and the destiny of the community, on the other hand. The dominant ideology believes, in its power and its wisdom,

that you can compartmentalize and privatize;
that you can declare unwelcome social reality inoperative and
    irrelevant;
that you can separate economics from neighborliness;
that you can enjoy chosenness and thereby avoid the demands
    of the others.

The prophets know better! They bear witness to the intransigent givens of God that are at the same time gift and trouble. Reality must be faced and not resisted. Their rhetoric is designed to break the bubble, to make contact with the facts on the ground — that God is here and neighbor is here — and to notice the links of chosenness in the present and future fates. It is no wonder that the ideologues thought that the prophets were crazy people (Hosea 9:7) and traitors (Jeremiah 38:4). It is no wonder that Jeremiah can dismiss his contemporary ideologues as false. He acknowledges them as false prophets whom God has not authorized:

I did not send the prophets,
    yet they ran;
I did not speak to them,
    yet they prophesied.

But if they had stood in my council,
    then they would have proclaimed my words to my people,
    and they would have turned them from their evil way,
        and from their evil doings. (Jeremiah 23:21-22)

Prophetic realism is always juxtaposed to ideological deception. The issue is joined with courage and freedom and sometime breaks the bubble of illusion.

III.

U.S. society is deeply committed, as was ancient Israel, to an ideology of exceptionalism. As with ancient Israel, that ideology could claim that the United States is a peculiar nation (people) in the world with a peculiar God-given mandate for democracy and freedom that would be pursued with messianic zeal. As with ancient Israel, moreover, that ideology of U.S. exceptionalism has brought with it a sense of entitlement and privilege and a distorted view of reality that continues to prevent us from seeing clearly how it is in the world of economic and political power over which God governs.

The roots of U.S. exceptionalism are very old and very deep, as lined out by Todd Gitlin and Liel Liebovitz in their important book, *The Chosen Peoples*.[10] It is common to find rootage for that self-understanding in the phrasing of John Winthrop, the Puritan governor who addressed the arriving Puritans that their new social reality with its new political-religious resolve would be "a city set upon a hill."[11] Winthrop opened the way for a sense of peculiar

10. Todd Gitlin and Liel Liebovitz, *The Chosen Peoples: America, Israel, and the Ordeals of Divine Election* (New York: Simon & Schuster, 2010).
11. Gitlin and Leibovitz, *The Chosen Peoples*, 66-67.

destiny that was God-given as the Puritans arrived at a new Promised Land to organize their public life in a new and faithful way. Since the time of the early Puritans, U.S. self-understanding has been saturated with biblical phrasing and allusion that portrayed the United States as God's chosen people.[12]

That combination of religion and politics has transposed variously into a passion both for democratic freedom and justice and for assertive expansionism in which the use of force is taken to be legitimate in the exercise of that destiny. In the delineation of that ideology by Gitlin and Liebovitz, we may note especially two poignant moments. First, Abraham Lincoln, in his characteristic way, acknowledged that sense of exceptionalism in his remarkable phrase "his almost chosen people," a phrase he used in his address to the New Jersey Senate on February 21, 1861.[13] Lincoln had enough of a sense of irony to know that the "almost" was a critical modifier that maintained a critical distance between the purposes of God and the self-understanding of his nation. That irony, of course, came to forceful expression in Lincoln's struggle with the issue of slavery, which no one in his time could any longer imagine to be the will of God.

But second, by the end of the nineteenth century, Lincoln's sense of irony had fully evaporated from the notion of U.S. exceptionalism. The great agent of transposing U.S. exceptionalism into aggressive imperial policy was Teddy Roosevelt. His leadership and his rhetoric, Gitlin and Liebovitz make clear, is less than noble:

12. On the continuing appeal of U.S. political rhetoric to the Mosaic narrative of election, see Bruce Feiler, *America's Prophet: Moses and the American Story* (New York: Morrow, 2009).

13. Gitlin and Liebovitz, *The Chosen Peoples*, 102-12. For the complete speech, see Abraham Lincoln, *Speeches and Writings, 1859-1865: Speeches, Letters, and Miscellaneous Writings, Presidential Messages and Proclamations* (New York: Literary Classics of the United States, 1989), 209-10. On Lincoln's appeal to Moses, see Feiler, *America's Prophet*, 160-68.

He preferred the allure of racial superiority, which filled the intellectual atmosphere in which he came of age. Such thinking, in the social Darwinist vein suffused the courses he took at Harvard (1876-1880) and Columbia (1880-1881). . . . For fully fifteen years, in the dominant tenor of his time, Roosevelt's historical writing was pervaded by talk of "Anglo-Saxonism" and "Aryan" as well as the then-fashionable "Teutonic" civilization. Later he would say that if he were rewriting his early books, he would not have used the term "Anglo-Saxon," calling it "an absurd name unless applied to the dominant race in England between the Fifth and the Eleventh Centuries." "Aryan," he would eventually conclude, was a linguistic description, not a biological one. In later years he gravitated towards the term "English-speaking races."[14]

The racist element in Roosevelt's thinking was of a piece with Andrew Jackson's expulsion of the Cherokee nation and the Trail of Tears, a considered U.S. policy in the claim of land for white Europeans who always have kept themselves on the alert for *Lebensraum*.[15]

The expansionist and racist elements of exceptionalism in the wake of President Theodore Roosevelt have been well narrated by James Bradley in his book *The Imperial Cruise*.[16] Bradley traces the manipulative game of foreign policy as the Roosevelt administration reached into the Pacific with the acquisition of the Philippines and into the affairs of Korea, Japan, and China all in the name of U.S. "Manifest Destiny" and with the conviction that the Asian peoples were inferior and needed such assistance in

14. Gitlin and Liebovitz, *The Chosen Peoples*, 115.

15. I use the term deliberately to allude to Hitler's annexation of territory under the claim that the German people needed "living space." The need and justification in the United States has not been very different from that.

16. James Bradley, *The Imperial Cruise: A Secret History of Empire and War* (New York: Little, Brown, 2009).

the administration of their national life. We may note in passing that Bradley exhibits a photograph of U.S. military personnel, already in 1901, "water boarding" a resistant Filipino![17] One can only conclude that exceptionalism eventually morphs into a self-serving policy of brutality that is justified with religious fervor, for chosenness becomes an excuse for self-assertion that in the end nourishes a violent society.

I need only add that 9/11 has evoked a torrent of commentary on the ideology of U.S. exceptionalism that I simply cite, a torrent of expression that is notable not only for its quantity, but for its shrewd discernment of the way in which arrogance, expansionism, racism, and violence have converged in a warrant for the unrestrained assertion of what is perceived as national interest. There is no doubt that 9/11 made it possible for us to imagine that our country, given its chosenness, is under assault because of our "passion for freedom." Such a notion is an irresistible way to conceal from ourselves our vigorous pursuit of natural resources and markets in ways that impinge upon the life of other nations and other cultures. That ideology serves exactly to justify the rightness of such actions as a national enterprise. The following are among the writers who have engaged that ideology, since 9/11, in a critical fashion:

- Mark Danner writes of "our state of exception" in which torture has become an acceptable practice and a legitimate policy:

  Meanwhile the one element that, since the early Roman dictatorship, all states of exception have shared — that they are temporary, that they end — seems lacking in ours. Ten years later, what was the exceptional has become the normal. The provisations of panic are the reality of our daily lives.[18]

17. Bradley, *The Imperial Cruise*, 107.
18. Mark Danner, "After September 11: Our State of Exception," *New York Review of Books*, October 13, 2011, 48.

- Gary Dorrien has probed the way in which exceptionalism has been co-opted by neoconservatives, coupled with their religious passion for being in control.[19]
- *The Atlantic*, in November 2007, offered a symposium on "The American Idea."[20] While a diversity of opinions are offered, what strikes the reader is that the exceptionalism of the United States is indeed an idea, an act of imagination that has been transposed into aggressive policy.
- Madeleine Albright, as reported by Michael Hardt and Antonio Negri, has declared:

> If we have to use force, it is because we are America. We are the indispensable nation.

Hardt and Negri comment on Albright's dictum that she allows for ambiguity, whether as an "exception from the corruption" or an "exception from the law." I suspect that we are mostly unclear about the matter.[21]

- Francis Fukuyama, after his season of hubris from which he has repented, considers the popular notion of "benevolent hegemony" on the part of the United States. He concludes that it is an unsustainable idea in the world of international politics.[22]

---

19. Gary Dorrien, "Consolidating the Empire: Neoconservatism and the Politics of American Dominion," *Political Theology* 6 (2005) 409-428. See also James W. Skillen, "Evangelicals and American Exceptionalism," *Review of Faith & International Affairs* 4/3 (Winter, 2006) 45-46.

20. "The Future of the American Idea," *Atlantic*, November, 2007, 13-62.

21. Michael Hardt and Antonio Negri, *Multitude: War and Democracy in the Age of Empire* (New York: Penguin, 2004), 8.

22. Francis Fukuyama, *America at the Crossroads: Democracy, Power, and the Neoconservative Legacy* (New Haven: Yale University Press, 2006), 111-13. Fukuyama is here much more persuasive than in his earlier, unfortunate rendering of *The End of History and the Last Man* (New York: Free Press, 1992).

- Godfrey Hodgson, in his book *The Myth of American Exceptionalism,* sees that the notion of exceptionalism has drawn us away from the reality that the U.S. is a country among others and must understand itself in that way.[23]
- James Carroll, writing in the wake of the death of Boris Yeltsin, has observed concerning the long contest between the U.S. and the USSR:

> There are many gods. In the United States, it was the god of American exceptionalism that failed. Even while standing firmly against the brutalities of Stalinism, this nation confronted its own capacity for self-betrayal, in nothing more dramatically than in the Vietnam War. . . . The era through which Boris Yeltsin lived teaches that there is no god but God whose absence is a presence.[24]

- Larry Rasmussen has considered the way in which Reinhold Niebuhr was an endless critic of U.S. Empire and the illusionary assumptions that sustain it.[25]
- Andrew Bacevich, in his book *The Limits of Power,* has for his subtitle *The End of American Exceptionalism.*[26] Bacevich brings to the question a strong measure of political realism and makes the practical judgment that such a posture is not sustainable in the real world of internationalism.

I cite this avalanche of data not to overwhelm, but only to indicate a) that the issue of U.S. exceptionalism is an urgent issue

23. Godfrey Hodgson, *The Myth of American Exceptionalism* (New Haven: Yale University Press, 2009).

24. James Carroll, "The Gods That Failed," *Boston Globe,* April 30, 2007.

25. Larry L. Rasmussen, "Reinhold Niebuhr," in *Empire and the Christian Tradition: New Readings of Classical Theologians,* ed. Kwok Pui-lan, Don H. Compier, and Joerg Rieger (Minneapolis: Fortress, 2007), 371-87.

26. Andrew Bacevich, *The Limits of Power: The End of American Exceptionalism* (New York: Holt, 2009).

among us, as it was in the ancient city of Jerusalem, and b) that the issue of exceptionalism is forcefully evoked by 9/11, in the same way it was evoked in that ancient world by the destruction of Jerusalem concerning the chosenness of Israel. I assume that for many readers this may pose no interesting question. And some will find my analogue to the Old Testament unpersuasive, upsetting, or irritating. I have no wish to confront or to persuade, but only to consider that in the interpretive trajectory of the prophetic tradition this is an issue that will not go away, one that requires of us our best critical, faithful thinking.

I make these observations about our deep conviction of exceptionalism that we have almost all come to share:

- The matter of exceptionalism in our society has now morphed into a broad and deep *militarism* that pervades our society.[27] That ideological insistence is evident everywhere among us, not least in the urge to have U.S. flags in our places of worship. Every pastor knows, moreover, that any critique of the U.S. military evokes great resistance. I submit that such resistance is surely a measure of the grip that the ideology of exceptionalism has upon us. That militarization of our society, in the name of security or of patriotism, serves to assure perpetual war in order to maintain supremacy in the world. That in turn leads to budgetary commitment that skews every other claim upon our national economy.
- The notion of U.S. exceptionalism has now morphed into *an oligarchy* in which power and money flow to a very few persons in our society. That oligarchy keeps most of the rest of us on board for the notion of chosenness, but only to the great

27. On the military permeation of our society, see Chalmers Johnson, *Blowback: The Costs and Consequences of American Empire* (New York: Holt, 2004); *The Sorrows of Empire: Militarism, Secrecy, and the End of the Republic* (New York: Holt, 2005).

benefit of the few who control government, the courts, and the media.[28]

· The ideology of exceptionalism continues to have *a racist component*. Since the "Teutonic" rhetoric of Teddy Roosevelt, our propensity is to regard others as inferior and incapable of wise government or mature culture — in his case it was the Asians; in our case it is the Mideast Muslims who we imagine are inferior to our own capacity in the world. And of course, that racism is closer home, so that "real Americans," unlike others among us including the President, are not really American.[29] The not subtle claim is that to be an American means to be of European stock.

· The ideology functions to sustain *our control of natural resources, markets, and supplies of cheap labor* in the rest of the world. The outsourcing of jobs to cheap labor markets serves the interest of the oligarchy that controls the flow of money, a control that is less and less interested in the maintenance and well-being of a democratic society. The continuing protest against regulation is in the interest of a predatory culture without restraint, much to the loss of most of our citizens. Larry Rasmussen has discerned the economic component of this ideology:

> If you wish to understand U.S. domestic and foreign policy since World War II, even World War I, and if you wish

28. The force of the ideology among those who cannot benefit from it is narrated by Thomas Frank, *What's the Matter with Kansas: How Conservatives Won the Heart of America* (New York: Holt, 2005).

29. Given Roosevelt's later repudiation of the term "Anglo-Saxon" as an "absurdity" for any contemporary application, it is astonishing that on the day I write this (July 25, 2012) one of the aides to Mitt Romney, in playing the race card against President Obama, has made the boastful claim that Mitt Romney is in sync with the "Anglo-Saxon" heritage of the U.S. The fact that such a phrase would be used indicates the extent to which the old racism on which Roosevelt traded is still potent and operative in our public life.

to know why the U.S. will seek to exercise imperial power for the foreseeable future, no matter who is president, you need understand only one thing: the exacting requirements of U.S. American affluence. Both Presidents Bush have said exactly the same thing, the first at the Earth Summit in 1992, the second after September 11, 2001: "The American way of life is not up for negotiation." They were not aberrant in this, or partisan. We will do all we need and can to keep the American way of life *as American Affluence* from the negotiating table. With our inordinate power, that means an imperial posture virtuously clad in an ideology of democratic capitalism, with freedom and prosperity the promise and the lure. Such prosperity is in fact the validation of faith, freedom, and free markets as the creed of a redeemer nation, indeed the creed of a righteous empire that does not understand its unrighteousness.[30]

When we consider the convergence of these factors — race, military adventurism, monopolized wealth, unsustainable affluence, and God-given destiny — it is clear enough that this ideology, as in ancient Israel, distorted reality. In ancient Jerusalem, they could not see the facts on the ground, so busy were they with their Songs of Zion. In a parallel way, we are so busy chanting "USA, USA," now our Song of Zion, that we do not notice:

- That the U.S. power is now limited and will become more so in the face of China;
- That the infrastructure of our society — schools, health care, universities, bridges, roads — is now deeply neglected, as our economy of greed drives money away from the common good;
- That the economy of the oligarchs, in the name of democratic

30. Rasmussen, "Reinhold Niebuhr," 385.

32

ideals, now skews and puts at risk the opportunity of very many people for a life of well-being.

To some great extent, I judge that our society lives in a bubble of illusion that is addicted to certain ideas that are remote from the lived reality that is all around us. In our situation, I judge, much like that of ancient Jerusalem, we are unable to see, to notice, or to take seriously the social reality in front of us. Amos, in that ancient world, chided his contemporaries, who engaged in illusionary self-indulgence but were not "grieved over the ruin of Joseph" (Amos 6:6). That is, they did not notice that their society was going to hell in a hand-basket!

IV.

The prophetic task, in our contemporary society as in ancient Jerusalem, is to counter the governing ideology, in both cases that of exceptionalism. The prophetic task is to expose the distorted view of societal reality sustained by the ideology that breeds unrealistic notions of entitlement, privilege, and superiority. Prophetic work in the wake of such exposé is to advocate and enact an alternative that refuses the illusion of the ideology and that takes seriously the reality of historical existence. As the destruction of Jerusalem was a wake-up call to historical reality that "chosenness" could not fend off, so 9/11 is a wake-up call to historical reality that the ideology of exceptionalism could not fend off among us.

From the perspective of Israel's prophetic tradition, the ideology of exceptionalism in Jerusalem seriously miscalculated on two fronts. First, it reduced YHWH to be patron of the dynasty and a guarantor of city and temple. It failed to acknowledge that YHWH is not simply a guarantor and patron, but is a lively character and active agent with a will and purpose other than that of the beneficiaries of the ideology (see Isaiah 55:8-9). In imagining its own ultimacy, the Jerusalem establishment had shelved the ultimacy of the God who will not be mocked and consequently had failed to recognize its own *pen*-ultimacy, its dependence upon and accountability to YHWH.

The inevitable and unsurprising consequence of such imagined ultimacy in the urban establishment of Jerusalem is arrogance that reduces YHWH to an object and therefore an irrelevance. Thus Zephaniah can say of the city:

> At that time I will search Jerusalem with lamps,
>   and I will punish the people
> who rest complacently on their dregs,
>   those who say in their hearts,
> "The Lord will not do good,
>   nor will he do harm." (Zephaniah 1:12)

This hubris, expressed as autonomy, imagined that the ones with power to do so could exploit in greedy and violent ways as they chose, taking advantage of the weak and vulnerable. Thus with Dostoyevsky, "Without God, everything is possible." So it was in Jerusalem, according to prophetic exposé. The prophetic indictment is consistent about the practice of injustice that is grounded in a disregard of the Torah of YHWH. The prophetic critique is to insist upon the ultimacy of YHWH that curbs such exploitation. YHWH, moreover, has so ordered creation that such abusive behavior has consequences that cannot be evaded.

Second, this sense of autonomy from God and unfettered freedom is exposed as disregard for the neighbor. The prophets, following the covenantal tradition of Deuteronomy, identify "widow, orphan, immigrant" as the visible representatives of the socially, economically vulnerable:

Learn to do good;
seek justice,
    rescue the oppressed,
defend the orphan,
    plead for the widow. (Isaiah 1:17)

They have grown fat and sleek.
They know no limits in deeds of wickedness;
    they do not judge with justice
the cause of the orphan, to make it prosper,
    and they do not defend the right of the needy.
                        (Jeremiah 5:28)

Father and mother are treated with contempt in you; the
alien residing within you suffers extortion; the orphan and
the widow are wronged in you. (Ezekiel 22:7)

The prophetic insistence is both theological and pragmatic. On
the one hand, abuse of the vulnerable neighbor is an affront to
God and a violation of Torah. On the other hand, in practical ways
such abuse is an unsustainable policy; in the act itself there arise
destructiveness and costly consequences for the body politic.

Thus exceptionalism as autonomy comes to violate the two
great commandments of love of God and love of neighbor. Exceptionalism imagines divine guarantees, so that one need not
answer to the divine will. The resultant entitlement depends upon
insensitivity to the need or even the presence of the neighbor. The
disregard of both God and neighbor permits a predatory society
to seem normal and acceptable.[31] And because it is situated in

---

31. On the destructive unrestrained acquisitive force of our society, see
Charles Ferguson, *Predator Nation: Corporate Criminals, Political Corruption, and
the Hijacking of America* (New York: Crown Business, 2012):

such an ideology, that "normal" predation comes to be beyond criticism.

The prophetic tradition, moreover, imagines an *alliance of God and neighbor* against such acquisitive exploitation, so that there is no possibility of loving God without loving neighbor. The apostolic witness of course affirms this linkage:

> Those who say, "I love God," and hate their brothers or sisters, are liars; for those who do not love a brother or sister whom they have seen, cannot love God whom they have not seen. (1 John 4:20)

But long before the epistle, Jeremiah had seen the convergence of God and neighbor:

> Did not your father eat and drink
> and do justice and righteousness?
> Then it was well with him.
> He judged the cause of the poor and needy;
> then it was well.
> Is this not to know me?
> says the LORD. (Jeremiah 22:15-16)

Care for the vulnerable is "knowledge of God." That prophetic formulation does not say that knowledge of God will lead to care for the neighbor; nor does it, alternatively, say that care for the vulnerable will lead to knowledge of God. Rather they are synonyms! The prophetic dictum, moreover, is in the context of an

---

If allowed to continue, this process will turn the United States into a declining, unfair society with an impoverished, angry, uneducated population under the control of a small, ultrawealthy elite. Such a society would be not only immoral, but eventually unstable, dangerously ripe for religious and political extremism. (p. 4)

indictment of King Jehoiakim for his practice of economic injustice and unrighteousness. The prophets know this already, as we are learning yet again, that dismissal of God and disregard of neighbor lead to disaster. So now our entitled predatory society imagines it is free of God's will and free to cast off neighbor without a safety net. And now we watch while our society unravels.

The matter is exceedingly difficult among us. We do not need to call this unraveling the judgment of God, because none of us wants to be an obscurantist supernaturalist about "the judgment of God." And yet, we have no other language with which to speak about the answerability that is intrinsic to the historical process, an answerability that exceptionalism wants to void.[32]

The task of the prophetic church, it follows, is to bear witness to *the irreducible reality of God* and *the irreducibility of the neighbor* as the reference points for a viable life in the world that even exceptionalism cannot nullify. In a society that has become increasingly "therapeutic," the viability of God as an ultimacy beyond our entitlements requires a kind of theological courage that is in short supply among us. But in truth the prophetic tradition has no ground on which to stand unless it can in some way attend to the holy ultimacy that lies beyond our canniest domestication.

While it is awkward at best to witness to such *divine ultimacy*,

---

32. Abraham Lincoln, in his Second Inaugural Address (*Speeches and Writings*, 687), given his deep sense of irony, found that the language of divine sovereignty worked effectively in public discourse:

> The Almighty has His own purposes. "Woe unto the world because of offences! for it must needs be that offences come; but woe to that man by whom the offence cometh!" If we shall suppose that American Slavery is one of these offences which, in the providence of God, must needs come, but which, having continued through His appointed time, He now wills to remove, and that He gives to both North and South, this terrible war, as the woe does to those by whom the offence came, shall we discern therein any departure from those divine attributes which the believers in a Living God always ascribe to Him?

it is easier and more characteristic for the prophetic church, both in neighborly practices and in policy advocacy, to focus on the presence and defining *importance of the neighbor,* most especially the neighbor who lives at the edge of or is excluded from the gifts of exceptionalism. The prophetic rhetoric abounds with language concerning covenantal neighborliness:

> Sow for yourselves righteousness;
>> reap steadfast love;
>> break up your fallow ground;
> for it is time to seek the LORD,
>> that he may come and rain righteousness upon you.
>> (Hosea 10:12)

> But as for you, return to your God,
>> hold fast to love and justice,
>> and wait continually for your God. (Hosea 12:6)

Do not oppress the widow, the orphan, the alien, or the poor; and do not devise evil in your hearts against one another. (Zechariah 7:10; see Amos 5:24; Micah 6:8; Jeremiah 9:23-24)

The terms — justice, righteousness, steadfast love — all concern neighborliness, and the tone is one of urgency! So it is in prophetic witness against the ideology exceptionalism. The prophets insist that there is an alternative that pertains to concrete socio-economic practice that must be undertaken just in the nick of time. It is very late for those who live in the illusion of ideology!

Such prophetic witness is sometimes abrasive and confrontational. We should, however, pay attention to the fact that the prophets characteristically spoke poetry. They proceeded by image, metaphor, and allusion that could not be reduced to a program and that could not be co-opted by the dominant ideology. At best prophetic testimony is not didactic or instructional; it is rather a bid for emancipatory faithful imagination, in the conviction that imagining outside the ideology will evoke fresh waves of energy and courage and generative obedience.[33]

We have exactly such ancient poetry in the face of ancient ideology. And now, among us, there is ample contemporary poetry that bears exactly the same witness. I cite the following as examples of how dominant ideology is challenged at the level of imagination. You may find these examples jarring or perhaps summoning for your own probes from outside and from beneath.

This is from Bud Osborn, a "poverty-rights activist" on "the street of the disenfranchised":

sad, lord
tired and worn
and sick
so sick
of power politics
of turf wars
of meetings and committees and subcommittees
sick of everything that loses
focus
because every deception
every agenda
every meeting
every resentment

---

33. This is the work of prophetic imagination that I have explored in *The Prophetic Imagination* (Minneapolis: Fortress, 1978) and *The Practice of Prophetic Imagination: Preaching an Emancipatory Word* (Minneapolis: Fortress, 2012).

every control grab
every move for money
slams down hardest
on the most wretched human beings
in north america
who are suffering and dying
in the streets and alleys and shit-hole hotels
of the downtown eastside
all the pettiness and ambition
slams directly down
on those who are most afflicted
by poverty and illness
addiction and discrimination
homelessness and demonizing propaganda . . .[34]

A second exemplar is from Julia Esquivel from Guatemala:

Each day false prophets
invited the inhabitants
of the Unchaste City
to kneel before the idols
of gluttony,
money,
and death:
Idolaters from all nations
were being converted to the American Way of Life.[35]

The walls of the Temples of Mammon
are like polished steel

---

34. Bud Osborn, *Hundred Block Rock* (Vancouver: Arsenal Pulp, 1999).
35. Julia Esquivel, *Threatened with Resurrection: Prayers and Poems from an Exiled Guatemalan* (2nd ed.; Elgin: Brethren, 1994), 81.

and in their windows
reality is distorted,
and so are the lights ignited
by the petroleum which its priests
have taken from the people
who now struggle for life and freedom
on the other side of the Rio Grande.[36]

In the most obscure and sordid place,
in the most hostile and harshest,
in the most corrupt
and nauseating places,
there You do Your work.
That is why Your Son
descended into hell,
in order to transform what IS NOT
and to purify that which IS BECOMING.
That is hope![37]

A third reading is from Wislawa Szymborska from Krakow,
Poland:

Nothing has changed.
The body still trembles as it trembled
before Rome was founded and after,
in the twentieth century before and after Christ.
Tortures are just what they were, only the earth has shrunk
and whatever goes on sounds as if it's just a room away.
Nothing has changed.
Except there are more people,

36. Julia Esquivel, *Threatened with Resurrection*, 85.
37. Julia Esquivel, *Threatened with Resurrection*, 105.

and new offenses have sprung up beside the old ones —
real, make-believe, short-lived, and nonexistent.
But the cry with which the body answers for them
was, is, and will be a cry of innocence
in keeping with the age-old scale and pitch.[38]

Finally, from Andrea Bieler and Luise Schrottroff as they ponder the Eucharist:

One cannot deny the bodily responses to starvation,
and that is part of the reason, some nights,
I sat in the basement of the dorm;
locked in a bathroom, catching myself in the mirror
as I stuffed candy bars, chips,
like a vending machine
anything into my mouth,
and then threw it up.
For while fifty million Americans
are currently dieting to lose weight,
nearly half that many are collecting food stamps
and/or standing in line at the local food pantry.[39]

And so
We witness today that God has put us in the center of this
        justice movement;
we witness today as so many have done before that we will
not turn back from this table of righteousness;
we recognize that when we witness the welcome of
        queer people,

38. Wislawa Szymborska, *Poems New and Collected 1957-1997*, trans. Stanislaw Barańczak and Clare Cavanagh (New York: Harcourt, Brace, 1998), 202.
39. Andrea Bieler and Luise Schrottroff, *The Eucharist: Bodies, Bread, & Resurrection* (Minneapolis: Fortress, 2007), 70.

when we put ourselves at the center of this communion,
we witness the welcome of all marginalized people;
we will witness to every denomination the river of justice
that is God's plan.[40]

Poetry that invites and transforms and shocks and offends may sometimes be the work of the Spirit. Our predatory society lives by prose that is manageable and thin. But then, the same was true with these ancient poets. They were odder than we usually credit them with being. The prophetic community knows that managed prose will often fend off the ultimacy of God and the quotidian presence of the neighbor. Such "fending off" will lead to death! But life wells up! It wells up outside the filtering space of our certitude. It shows itself among the unqualified. It yields fresh words and images and worlds, refusing our ideological masters. It is the "yet" that sounds after the triple "though" of death. Listen to this from Habakkuk:

Though the fig tree does not blossom,
and no fruit is on the vines;
though the produce of the olive fails
and the fields yield no food;
though the flock is cut off from the fold
and there is no herd in the stalls,
yet I will rejoice in the LORD;
I will exult in the God of my salvation. (Habakkuk 3:17-18)

Ideology does not get the "yet" that is given when the prophets speak!

---

40. Bieler and Schrottroff, *The Eucharist*, 129.

III

Grief amid Denial

Dying isn't hard.
What is hard is relinquishing.

CHRIS GRAHAM,
AS HE GOES DEEPLY INTO ALS

The end came upon the city of Jerusalem, even as the poets had long anticipated. Already one hundred and fifty years before, Amos had declared:

> **The end** has come upon my people Israel;
> I will never again pass them by.
> The songs of the temple shall become wailings on that day,
>   says the LORD God;
> the dead bodies shall be many,
> cast out in every place. Be silent! (Amos 8:2-3)

And after him, Jeremiah had uttered many words about an ending. His poetry is on a grand scale describing the dismantling of all creation:

> I looked on the earth, and lo, it was waste and void;
>   and to the heavens, and they had no light.

44

I looked on the mountains, and lo, they were quaking,
    and all the hills moved to and fro.
I looked, and lo, there was no one at all,
    and all the birds of the air had fled.
I looked, and lo, the fruitful land was a desert,
    and all its cities were laid in ruin
    before the Lord, before his fierce anger. . . .
Because of this the earth shall mourn,
    and the heavens above grow black;
for I have spoken, I have purposed;
    I have not relented nor will I turn back.
                              (Jeremiah 4:23-26, 28)

The prophets had anticipated, not predicted. They had anticipated because they knew that a public life out of sync with the will of the creator God could finally not be sustained.

Of course the ending was complex. Perhaps it was, as the prophets had said in their elusive poetry, the judgment of God. Or perhaps it was the inexorable outcome of policies of abuse and exploitation in which widows, orphans, and immigrants — the canaries of any social system — had suffered enough. Or perhaps the destruction was simply the consequence of Babylonian expansionism at the expense of a weaker state.

In any case, the end did come with great force and brutality. Along with the physical suffering, there was the deep humiliation of having the symbols of God's presence taken away in disrespect and treated as commodities:

The bronze pillars that were in the house of the Lord, as well as the stands and the bronze sea that were in the house of the Lord, the Chaldeans broke into pieces, and carried the bronze to Babylon. They took away the pots, the shovels, the snuffers, the dishes for incense, and all the bronze vessels

used in the temple service, as well as the firepans and the
basins. What was made of gold the captain of the guard took
away for the gold, and what was made of silver, for the silver. As for the two pillars, the one sea, and the stands, which
Solomon had made for the house of the LORD, the bronze of
all these vessels was beyond weighing. The height of the one
pillar was eighteen cubits, and on it was a bronze capital;
the height of the capital was three cubits; latticework and
pomegranates, all of bronze, were on the capital around. The
second pillar had the same, with the latticework. (2 Kings
25:13-17)

Or as the Psalm describes the disrespectful seizure of the temple:

> At the upper entrance they hacked
>   the wooden trellis with axes.
> And then, with hatchets and hammers,
>   they smashed all its carved work.
> They set your sanctuary on fire;
>   they desecrated the dwelling place of your name,
>   bringing it to the ground.
> They said to themselves, "We will utterly subdue them";
>   they burned all the meeting places of God in the land.
> We do not see our emblems. . . . (Psalm 74:5-9)

All of this was anticipated; all this came to pass.

But the urban elites clustered around king and temple had
not seen it coming. They imagined that their life was so good, so
successful, and so guaranteed that it would not be interrupted.

I.

The practitioners of the ideology of exceptionalism in Jerusalem — chosen city, chosen king, chosen temple — lived in a state of denial about their coming future. Ideology as false consciousness does that to us. It gives us a constructed, contained view of reality that covers over the facts on the ground and offers us instead a preferred set of facts that reassures and confirms the way we thought and wished the world were. When the ideology is one of assurance issuing in entitlement and privilege, it will not be interrupted by facts on the ground, for such facts are characteristically "inconvenient." As a consequence, the facts on the ground must be denied in order to sustain a world view of entitlement and privilege.

In the broad sweep of Old Testament faith, I suggest that Job's friends in the book of Job are the quintessential deniers. They were convinced of a view of the moral calculus of the world that would account for everything. That moral calculus was vigorously voiced in the book of Deuteronomy, which affirmed that Torah obedience would result in God's blessings and Torah disobedience would bring God's judgment:

> See, I set before you today life and prosperity, death and adversity. If you obey the commandments of the LORD your God that I am commanding you today, by loving the LORD your God, walking in his ways, and observing his commandments, decrees, and ordinances, then you shall live and become numerous, and the LORD your God will bless you in the land that you are entering to possess. But if your heart turns away and you do not hear, but are led astray to bow down to other gods and serve them, I declare to you today that you will surely perish. (Deuteronomy 30:15-18; see 1 Kings 9:4-7)

That same view, moreover, was popularly voiced in Psalm 1, the teaching tool for Torah in which it is affirmed that Torah keepers prosper and Torah violators perish:

> The LORD watches over the way of the righteous,
> but the way of the wicked will perish. (Psalm 1:6)

And behind Deuteronomy and the covenantal traditions were the observations of the wisdom teachers in the book of Proverbs. They could see that wise choices begat well-being and foolish choices produced trouble.

Job's friends brought those assumptions to the deep moral, spiritual, theological crisis of Job and worked, in their commentary, to fit him into their calculus. This required them to deny the reality of Job's life, a denial that Job eventually refuses.

But the denial practiced in Jerusalem was of another ilk. There the certitude did not concern a covenantal *quid pro quo*. Exactly the opposite! It concerned, rather, an unconditional guarantee of divine favor and protection. That claim is given to David in the Nathan oracle:

> Your house and your kingdom shall be made sure **forever** before me; your throne shall be established **forever.** (2 Samuel 7:16)

The assurance is reiterated to Solomon in liturgical celebration:

> The LORD has said that he would dwell in thick darkness.
> I have built you an exalted house,
> a place for you to dwell in **forever.** (1 Kings 8:12-13)

That unconditional assurance is reinforced by the modifier — for the king, "forever," and the temple, "forever and ever." Nothing bad could happen here!

That liturgic assurance, moreover, was reinforced by the historical experience of Jerusalem at the end of the eighth century when the holy city was inexplicably (miraculously?) delivered from the threat of the Assyrian army. Isaiah had uttered the promise of YHWH to guarantee the city:

> Therefore thus says the LORD concerning the king of Assyria: He shall not come into this city, shoot an arrow there, come before it with a shield, or cast up a siege ramp against it. By the way that he came, by the same he shall return; he shall not come into this city, says the LORD. For I will defend this city to save it, for my own sake and for the sake of my servant David. (Isaiah 37:33-35)

It is for the sake of David, looking back to the oracle of 2 Samuel 7. But it is also for YHWH's own sake, that is, for the sake of God's reputation. The oracle of unconditional guarantee is validated in historical experience. It is a visible guarantee that nothing bad could happen here. It turns out that this wondrous rescue became great grist for Jerusalem's ideology. As YHWH delivered, so YHWH will endlessly deliver:

> Be not dismayed, whate'er betide,
> God will take care of you!

That remarkable rescue was at the end of the eighth century, 701 B.C.E. As the city moved into the seventh century (the 600s), the ideology of exceptionalism took on fresh force as the poetic anticipation of trouble for the city intensified in the poetry of Jeremiah, and so the ideology of exceptionalism with its required denial became more intense. The unconditional divine promises took on more and more force.

The prophetic tradition quotes back to the city its mantras of denial. The favorite slogan of the ideology of exceptionalism is the term "shalom." This is the name of the great king of well-being, "Solomon." It is the name of the chosen city — with a prefix, Jeru-"salem." The city is all about "shalom," a coherent system of well-being that is generative and sustainable. Never mind that the guaranteed system of shalom is organized on behalf of the elite and at the expense of the peasants. The shalom-ideology encompassed everything, so that every public official and every opinion-maker could speak of shalom. And now the prophet speaks it back to the city.

The prophetic indictment of Jeremiah 6:13-15 has at its center a quotation (or an alleged quotation) from official liturgy:

> For from the least to the greatest of them,
>   everyone is greedy for unjust gain;
> and from prophet to priest,
>   everyone deals falsely.
> They have treated the wound of my people carelessly,
>   saying, **"Peace, peace,"**
>   when there is no peace.
> They acted shamefully, they committed abomination;
>   yet they were not ashamed,
>   they did not know how to blush.
> Therefore they shall fall among those who fall;
>   at the time that I punish them, they shall be overthrown,
>   says the LORD.

The prophetic accusation concerns greedy exploitation that includes the entire leadership of the urban elite. They are so self-contained in their actions and their policies that they have no capacity for criticism, so unaware are they of what they do. They are, then, unable to blush, feeling no shame, so narcoticized that they have no sense of embarrassment about their way of life.

Such a practice, says the poet, leads to a defining "therefore" of inescapable consequences. They will fall and be overthrown, even though they think themselves secure.

At the center of this indictment is this potent statement:

They say, "shalom, shalom."

They say it in public assurance and in liturgic mantra. They declare a state of guaranteed well-being, as though it could be established by fiat. But, says the poet, such mantras of self-confidence and self-congratulations in fact are contradicted by reality. There is no such shalom. There is no state of well-being. But that reality lies beyond the purview of the ideologues. The ideology could not tolerate such an awareness, so no such acknowledgement.

This poetic utterance with a mocking quote at its center is so important that it is reiterated in Jeremiah 8:10-12, only this time the concluding "therefore" is matched by an introductory "therefore," making the danger to the urban elite even more acute:

> **Therefore** I will give their wives to others
>   and their fields to conquerors,
> because from the least to the greatest
>   everyone is greedy for unjust gain:
> from prophet to priest
>   everyone deals falsely.
> They have treated the wound of my people carelessly,
>   saying, "Peace, peace,"
>   when there is no peace.
> They acted shamefully, they committed abomination;
>   yet they were not at all ashamed,
>   they did not know how to blush.
> **Therefore** they shall fall among those who fall;
>   at the time when I punish them, they shall be overthrown.

The intent is the same: unjust greed by the leadership, inability to blush in embarrassment because all norms of responsible propriety have been nullified. It is the same prospect of fall and overthrow, but now wives and fields are given to others, i.e., to invading forces. That word pair "wives and fields" incorporates terms not unlike those of the tenth commandment: "Do not covet your neighbor's field or wife" (Deuteronomy 5:21!). But now in anticipation, it is all lost, because of a denying, illusionary "shalom, shalom."

Jeremiah is echoed more graphically by his contemporary Ezekiel. Here it is an indictment of the religious leadership that has offered phony assurances right out of the ideology of exceptionalism:

> My hand will be against the prophets who see false visions and utter lying divinations. (Ezekiel 13:9)

Their affront:

> Because, in truth, because they have misled my people, saying, **"Peace,"** when there is no peace; and because, when the people build a wall, these prophets smear whitewash on it. (v. 10)

The people build a wall of denial, a facade of policy. But the religious leaders do the "whitewash." They provide the slogans and the mantras and link the whole to God in order to provide false assurances that cover over illegitimate policies. No doubt the leadership types believed those liturgic assurances: All will be well! All manner of things will be well, because God has promised!

The theological failure of the religious leadership consists in debilitating the character of God. In the old covenantal tradition, God was indeed an active agent with whom to reckon. But as the urban economy flourished, as the urban elites became more affluent and with it more intellectually sophisticated, such a notion of divine agency became less and less palatable, more intellectually embarrassing, and more politically inconvenient. Without ever being explicit, the wild rawness of divine agency simply disappeared into smoother liturgical formulation. Now the God who had been an agent who took initiatives became an object to be adored. Now the God who was the subject of verbs is on the receiving end of religion, made innocuous and eventually irrelevant to life. The ideology is a closed case that does not want a disruptive agent on the horizon. The God of Sinai is reformulated as the patron of Zion.

Thus Jeremiah can say of the prophets of the house of Judah:

> They have spoken falsely of the Lord,
>   and have said, "He will do nothing.
> No evil will come upon us,
>   and we shall not see sword or famine." (5:12)

They have articulated a God who will not act. This God is so completely situated in the ideology of exceptionalism that this God will take no action against the establishment. God will not do evil, will not bring covenant sanctions. The city will never receive the covenant curses of sword (war) or famine, and perhaps implied "pestilence," the sum of "the big three." The covenantal tradition knew about the threat of "sword, famine, and pestilence," and Jeremiah had spoken about such a threat to the city:

> Those destined for pestilence, to pestilence,
>   and those destined for the sword, to the sword;
> those destined for famine, to famine,
>   and those destined for captivity, to captivity. (15:2)

But not in the exempt city! Jeremiah can say of such "adjusted" theology:

> The prophets are nothing but wind,
>   for the word is not in them.
> Thus it shall be done to them! (5:13)

They are nothing but wind! Jeremiah saw that they had said that God would not do evil. But Zephaniah, his contemporary, goes further:

> ... those who say in their hearts,
> "The Lord will not do good,
>   nor will he do harm." (Zephaniah 1:12)

Not only no evil, but no good either! God is completely eliminated as a player. All that is left is an abiding guarantee. No action, no disruption, no risk, just "forever"!

The defining narrative of denial is that of Hananiah in Jeremiah 27-28. His name means "YHWH is gracious." He is a professional prophet in Jerusalem. He seems, moreover, to be an heir to Isaiah. A century earlier Isaiah had assured King Hezekiah that God would save the city. And now, in the time of Jeremiah, as the crisis is evidently much more acute for the city, Hananiah reiterates the assurances of Isaiah. Only now a century later, everything is changed. One cannot simply repeat old mantras; new circumstances require new utterances. Hananiah is something of a "strict constructionist" who wants to reiterate without doing the hard work of contextual interpretation. And so he is engaged by his contemporary, Jeremiah, who is a master of powerful, honest, direct contextual interpretation.

The narrative concerning these two comes just after Babylon

had made its first incursion into Jerusalem and had exiled the king. Jeremiah is instructed by YHWH to make a yoke and wear it in public as a sign of the imperial imposition of Babylon, for a yoke signifies occupation, exploitation, and taxation:

> But if any nation or kingdom will not serve this king, Nebuchadnezzar of Babylon, and put its neck under the yoke of the king of Babylon, then I will punish that nation with the sword, with famine, and with pestilence, says the Lord, until I have completed its destruction by his hand. . . . But any nation that will bring its neck under the yoke of the king of Babylon and serve him, I will leave on its own land, says the Lord, to till it and live there. (Jeremiah 27:8-11)

The declaration concerns Nebuchadnezzar; but it is YHWH who acts! It is YHWH the creator who wills Babylonian conquest. And if the state will not submit to this dazzling superpower, it will receive sword, famine, and pestilence. The Jeremiah tradition affirms the agency of YHWH against Jerusalem in a way that will violate exceptionalism.

But in chapter 28 Hananiah, the prophet of Jerusalem exceptionalism, challenges Jeremiah's reading of reality. He is guided by exceptionalism, informed by Isaiah, and anticipates a speedy return to normalcy:

> Thus says the Lord of hosts, the God of Israel: I have broken the yoke of the king of Babylon. Within two years I will bring back to this place all the vessels of the Lord's house, which King Nebuchadnezzar of Babylon took away from this place and carried to Babylon. I will also bring back to this place King Jeconiah son of Jehoiakim of Judah, and all the exiles from Judah who went to Babylon, says the Lord, for I will break the yoke of the king of Babylon. (28:2-4)

The yoke of the empire cannot last, because this is Jerusalem with all its guarantees. The exiles from 598 B.C.E. will return! The deposed King Jehoiachin will be restored! All will be well! Jeremiah's response of incredulity at the words of Hananiah is just right:

> Amen! May the LORD do so; may the LORD fulfill the words that you have prophesied, and bring back to this place from Babylon the vessels of the house of the LORD, and all the exiles. (v. 6)

But then he counters the expectation of Hananiah with the old tradition of covenant:

> But listen now to this word that I speak in your hearing and in the hearing of all the people. The prophets who preceded you and me from ancient times prophesied war, famine, and pestilence against many countries and great kingdoms. As for the prophet who prophesies peace, when the word of that prophet comes true, then it will be known that the LORD has truly sent the prophet. (vv. 7-9)

In the street theatre that follows, Hananiah breaks the symbolic yoke of Jeremiah, bespeaking the breaking of the yoke of Babylon and again asserting normalcy in two years.

Jeremiah's immediate counter is to reappear with an iron yoke that cannot be broken, bespeaking the iron grip of Babylon on Jerusalem:

> Go, tell Hananiah, Thus says the LORD: You have broken wooden bars only to forge iron bars in place of them! (v. 13)

Thus the issue is joined. The narrative goes on to report that Hananiah died in the seventh month (v. 17). But the narrative is not interested in him. What matters is his endorsement of denial, his refusal to see the world that is in front of him, his inability to see that the God of rigorous requirement is on the scene. His ideological reductionism could not countenance such a God. He is not a lone voice in his society. He is in fact a representative of the conviction of the city that a quick return to normalcy would surely happen. Evidence to the contrary did not count. He was overruled by a conviction that made it impossible to see the reality at hand.

II.

The prophetic counter to denial rooted in the ideology of exceptionalism is the practice of grief that acknowledges loss — an acknowledgement that summons the city to be fully, deeply, and knowingly engaged in its actual life experience. The urban elite, of course, do not weep. Their ideology requires that they "suck it up" and move on. But their sense of loss lingers beneath what is acknowledged; it has, however, no compelling power to transform as long as it remains unacknowledged. For that reason, the prophetic counter of grief expressed may be an antidote to denial.

The prophets employ many varied rhetorical strategies in an attempt to break the denial. Of course, there is anger that purports to mirror the "wrath of God." There is much righteous indignation, that is, indignation that is voiced in the service of righteous solidarity with the vulnerable. I have come to think, however, that our usual assumptions about prophetic righteous indignation are overblown and mistaken, both because such speech is not seen as a rhetorical strategy rather than an unrestrained tirade, and because there are many other rhetorical strategies utilized as well. Here I will consider the way in which grief functions as

a rhetorical strategy a) in anticipation, b) in God's own performance, and c) finally in the actual life of Jerusalem.

Much of the prophetic poetry is an anticipation of the coming
loss of Jerusalem. The prophets knew well ahead of time that a
socio-economic system out of sync with YHWH's will for neighborliness cannot endure. Well ahead of the actual demise, these
prophets engage in an emotive performance of that which is not
yet available to the urban elites. Thus Amos, in his declaration
of "the end," anticipates a response to the loss. In the very temple (big house) where doxologies had been sung, there will be
weeping:

"The songs of the temple shall become wailings in that day,"
    says the Lord GOD;
"the dead bodies shall be many,
    cast out in every place. Be silent!" . . .
On that day, says the Lord GOD,
    I will make the sun go down at noon,
    and darken the earth in broad daylight.
I will turn your feasts into mourning,
    and all your songs into lamentation;
I will bring sackcloth on all loins,
    and baldness on every head;
I will make it like the mourning for an only son,
    and the end of it like a bitter day. (Amos 8:3, 9-10)

In his indictment of the urban elite for coveting and confiscation,
Micah can imagine the dread response to be made to loss:

On that day they shall take up a taunt song against you,
    and wail with bitter lamentation,
and say, "We are utterly ruined;
    the LORD alters the inheritance of my people;

how he removes it from me!
Among our captors he parcels out our fields." (Micah 2:4)

His anticipation is echoed by Zephaniah:

On that day, says the LORD,
a cry will be heard from the Fish Gate,
a wail from the Second Quarter,
a loud crash from the hills.
The inhabitants of the Mortar wail,
for all the traders have perished;
all who weigh out silver are cut off. (Zephaniah 1:10-11)

The poetic anticipation is shocking, because it is offered in a context that still seems to be well-functioning. The cry to come is a contradiction of what was visible to the established practice of ideology. Exceptionalism assured that it could not happen here. But the poets show that it could, indeed, that it would come here.

Of course, the great voice of grief is that of Jeremiah. He weeps, not because he is an emotional wreck, but because he already sees clearly the coming disaster that will not be averted. Among his poetic scenarios, I cite two. In 4:19-20, Jeremiah anticipates a scene in which the urban elites, asleep secure in their bedrooms, are shocked to see before their very eyes an invading soldier. The imagined appearance of a threatening soldier, a genuine nightmare, evokes anxiety:

My anguish, my anguish! I writhe in pain!
Oh, the walls of my heart!
My heart is beating wildly;
I cannot keep silent;
for I hear the sound of the trumpet,

the alarm of war.
Disaster overtakes disaster,
    the whole land is laid waste.
Suddenly my tents are destroyed,
    my curtains in a moment. (Jeremiah 4:19-20)

The poet sounds the alarm of an invading army, right in the midst of a viable, seemingly secure society. The reason for the contradiction between assumed security and unnoticed threat is that the urban elites are completely narcoticized by ideology and cannot see:

For my people are foolish,
    they do not know me;
they are stupid children,
    they have no understanding.
They are skilled in doing evil,
    but do not know how to do good. (v. 22)

In a second scenario, the poet imagines that the city has become a whore on the street, looking desperately for a partner, but in fact in deep danger, a danger that remains unacknowledged:

And you, O desolate one,
what do you mean that you dress in crimson,
    that you deck yourself with ornaments of gold,
    that you enlarge your eyes with paint?
In vain you beautify yourself.
    Your lovers despise you;
    they seek your life. (Jeremiah 4:30)

But in verse 31, the imagery shifts from an alluring prostitute to a cry like a woman in labor, vulnerable and in deep pain. The abrupt change of image is an attempt to rattle and destabilize the illusion of the city:

> For I heard a cry as of a woman in labor,
>   anguish as one of bringing forth her first child,
> the cry of daughter Zion gasping for breath,
>   stretching out her hands,
> "Woe is me! I am fainting before killers!" (v. 31)

In a quick reversal, ornament is reduced to vulnerability and beauty to desperation. All of this is to come, even upon those who imagine themselves safe and immune.

In the remarkable poem of 8:18–9:2, the poet grieves over "my poor people" (8:19, 21; 9:1). The poet speaks; but because it is YHWH who refers to Israel as "my poor people," it is credible to consider that it is YHWH who weeps over the city that is soon coming to ruin. On that reading, it is YHWH who has a sick heart. It is YHWH who hears the wonderment of Israel in 8:19. It is YHWH who hears the resignation of Jerusalem in 8:20. It is YHWH who can say:

> Is there no balm in Gilead?
>   Is there no physician there?
> Why then has the health of my poor people
>   not been restored? (8:22)

Perhaps verse 22 voices divine bewilderment. There is available balm. There are accessible doctors. But there is no healing. There is no restoration. And so the question: Why? No answer is given. Rather, in 9:1-2 there is an emotional collapse, because the unspoken truth is acknowledged. What YHWH knows — and Jeremiah knows — is that the city is beyond rescue. The available medicine and doctors are not adequate to the crisis:

They bend their tongues like bows;
    they have grown strong in the land for falsehood,
      and not for truth;
  for they proceed from evil to evil,
    and they do not know me, says the LORD. (9:3)

YHWH wants to flee the scene, unbearable as it is. The poet can portray YHWH at wits' end, ready to "leave my people," wanting to be elsewhere, to "weep day and night." The poet throws such imagery in the face of obdurate, unnoticing Jerusalem which, in its denial, is out of reach of the tears of acknowledgement.

Then these three segments in chapter 9:

- In verses 10-11, the poetry presents a severe drought:

  Take up weeping and wailing for the mountains,
    and a lamentation for the pastures of the wilderness,
  because they are laid waste so that no one passes through,
    and the lowing of cattle is not heard;
  both the birds of the air and the animals
    have fled and are gone.
  I will make Jerusalem a heap of ruins,
    a lair for jackals,
  and I will make the towns of Judah a desolation,
    without inhabitant.

The drought is enough to cause the undoing of creation, not unlike global warming (see 4:23-26; Hosea 4:3). The collapse of the ecosystem will mean disaster for the city, sure to become a place of abandonment. The coming disaster is a "natural" disaster. Such a disaster of course can be explained in "natural" terms concerning the abuse of the ecosystem. At the same time, however, the covenantal tradition in which Jeremiah stands knows very well that such a "covenant curse" is the work of the God of the covenant who will not be mocked. These verses, however, do not even mention God. The drought, rather, is the outworking of the way in which the city has organized social power, a way of organization that is unsustainable, resulting in the devastation of the city itself.

• As consequence, the poet imagines that such a crisis requires the grieving resources of society (9:17-19). Juliana Claassens has considered the way in which the women skilled in grief are necessary to "performing" the death of the city.[1] She calls these women, after the Old Irish usage, "keeners," the women who have the skills, courage, and presence to bring any death to speech, so that the community can fully and finally embrace the loss.

Now Jeremiah asserts that the city itself requires such "keeners" because the city is coming to its death:

Thus says the LORD of hosts:
Consider, and call for the mourning women to come;
   send for the skilled women to come;
let them quickly raise a dirge over us,
   so that our eyes may run down with tears,
   and our eyelids flow with water. (vv. 17-18)

The work of the women is to "perform" the death. And beyond the women, imagines the poet, Zion itself wails, in an echo of the lines I have cited from Amos and Micah:

1. L. Juliana M. Claassens, *Mourner, Mother, Midwife: Reimagining God's Delivering Presence in the Old Testament* (Louisville: Westminster John Knox, 2013), ch. 2.

For a sound of wailing is heard from Zion:
"How we are ruined!
We are utterly shamed,
because we have left the land,
because they have cast down our dwellings." (v. 19)

The vigorous rhetoric of loss answers ruin, abandonment, and being "cast down." The verse is dominated by "we," we the urban elite in the city,

We are ruined,
We are utterly ashamed,
We have departed the land.

It is as though the denial of being "Not ashamed" (6:15; 8:12) has been broken, overpowered by events. Finally, the last phrase refers to "they," presumably the Babylonian army. It is as though at the last desperate moment, the inhabitants of the city have seen reality. That reality is that in the real world, the ideology of chosenness will not protect the city. The army will come here in devastation. The cry is because of a newly discerned risk and vulnerability, as though the entire facade of protection has dissolved. The loss is now real, embraced, and acknowledged. But even here, God is not mentioned. The immediacy of reality does not require theological commentary. It is enough to face the reality of utter loss and abandonment.

- The urgency of the death scene is escalated even further in 9:20-22:

  Hear, O women, the word of the LORD,
      and let your ears receive the word of his mouth;
  teach to your daughters a dirge

64

and each to her neighbor a lament.
"Death has come up into our windows,
    it has entered our palaces,
to cut off the children from the streets
    and the young men from the squares."
Speak! Thus says the LORD:
"Human corpses shall fall
    like dung on the open field,
like sheaves behind the reaper,
    and no one shall gather them."

The poetry is addressed, ostensibly, to the "keeners." They have urgent work to do. The urgency is because "death" has entered the most protected places. Death is personified, treated as an active agent who is able to penetrate the best security systems of the urban elite. This devastating agent of negation has come through the guarded windows of the palaces, has broken through the security systems of the mansions, has seeped through the vaults of the great investment banks, has broken open the secrets of the military, has assaulted the children who have been most protected, and is after the "young men," the prize of this patriarchal society. Everything is at risk. Everyone is under threat. Now it is not an army. It is not even YHWH. It is the last, elusive enemy who will undo all that is treasured. According to the poet, moreover, death does not pause to honor chosenness. The outcome, says the poet, is a heap of bodies, like the work of terrorists who indiscriminately destroy without regard or respect, leaving waste in a field like sheaves of grain, scattered randomly, left without attention.

The poet is relentless in drawing the future of the city down to "ground zero." This is not a poem about the anger of YHWH. It is rather a scenario of the most elemental, most unthinkable, most unutterable vulnerability that moves beneath reasonableness and that defies explanation in order to voice vulnerability and loss at the deepest level. The poetry is unrelieved. The urgency is not eased. There is no escape!

All of this is an anticipation. It is anticipated that ruin will come, that YHWH will grieve, that death will be on the loose, that the city will sink into helplessness. And then, it is as though the denial has been penetrated. The city can no longer "suck it up," because the stench of death given in the poetry is too powerful and unbearable. And so finally the deep grief of loss comes to the lips of the city too long in denial.

- It is as though the glorious "songs of Zion" (e.g., Psalm 46) have been transposed into the "Dirges of Zion." These psalms, unlike the prophetic words, are not anticipation. They are acknowledgements after fact. But they are acknowledgements!

Psalm 74 is a bid for divine attention *in extremis*. The Psalm culminates in a passionate petition that YHWH should act, that God should be faithful toward Israel and deal with the perpetration of violence against the city:

> Do not deliver the soul of your dove to the wild animals;
>> do not forget the life of your poor forever.
> Have regard for your covenant,
>> for the dark places of the land are full of the haunts
>> of violence.
> Do not let the downtrodden be put to shame;
>> let the poor and needy praise your name.
> Rise up, O God, plead your cause;
>> remember how the impious scoff at you all day long.
> Do not forget the clamor of your foes,
>> the uproar of your adversaries that goes up continually.
>> (Psalm 74:19-23)

In its loss, Israel can still speak urgent petitions to YHWH. The ground for petition is laid in the preceding verses. On the one hand, the loss is described in detail, as though to say to YHWH, "We get it!" (vv. 1-11). We get the loss. We get the fact that our chosenness has not protected us. We get that we are vulnerable and that we are dependent.

But on the other hand, in loss Israel can still appeal to God's attachment to the city. This is

your pasture (v. 1),
your congregation (v. 2),
your heritage (v. 2).
your holy place (v. 4)
the dwelling place of your name (v. 7).

Israel has no claim to make for itself.

But it does, in its loss, make a claim for God. While Israel has no ground for self-assertion, it bids YHWH to remember YHWH's own capacity. With the disruptive conjunction of verse 12 (rendered as "yet"), Israel recalls, for YHWH, YHWH's manifest power, seeking to mobilize that power on behalf of Israel. In its deep loss, Israel can remember that the loss pertains only to itself, not to YHWH. YHWH has lost nothing of YHWH's capacity for governance, for this is the creator who has all reality in purview, including even "Leviathan" (vv. 12-17). Even the force of death is no match for this Lord of orderly life. Now Israel, in its loss and vulnerability, can fall back on the power and fidelity of YHWH.

- The grief comes to speech among the elite who were deported to Babylon. Thus the displaced remembered and wept:

  By the rivers of Babylon —
      there we sat down and there we wept. (Psalm 137:1)

This is perhaps a nostalgic look backward:

> If I forget you, O Jerusalem,
>   let my right hand wither!
> Let my tongue cling to the roof of my mouth,
>   if I do not remember you,
> if I do not set Jerusalem above my highest joy. (vv. 5-6)

But the cry for vengeance is an act of trust (vv. 7-9). These speakers know that at bottom the one who gave them life can still be addressed, even if the address is shameless in its hunger for retaliation. The phrasing of grief must have been familiar, for in a different context, Nehemiah can say the same words of grief:

> "The survivors there in the province who escaped captivity are in great trouble and shame; the wall of Jerusalem is broken down, and its gates have been destroyed by fire." When I heard these words I sat down and wept, and mourned for days, fasting and praying before the God of heaven. (Nehemiah 1:3-4)

To "sit down and weep" is to let the loss flow over one.[2] It is a complete acknowledgement without denial. It is, moreover, on the basis of that full disclosure of loss that Nehemiah can promptly take a new action for the future, and recruit the resources of the empire toward rebuilding (Nehemiah 2:1-8).

- The grief among the elite deportees is matched by the grief of the "lesser" folk who remained in the bereft land (see 2 Kings 25:12). From them comes the book of Lamentations, the full

---

2. See Kenneth J. Doka, ed., *Disenfranchised Grief: New Directions, Challenges, and Strategies for Practice* (Champaign: Research, 2002).

voicing of grief, the complete acknowledgement of loss, and the total embrace of vulnerability, everything from A to Z. The poems in the book of Lamentations give full expression to loss. There is no more denial:

> How lonely sits the city
>   that once was full of people!
> How like a widow she has become,
>   she that was great among the nations!
> She that was a princess among the provinces
>   has become a vassal.
> She weeps bitterly in the night,
>   with tears on her cheeks;
> among all her lovers
>   she has no one to comfort her;
> all her friends have dealt treacherously with her,
>   they have become her enemies. (Lamentations 1:1-2)

This is a full acknowledgement that the abandoned city is now without a "comforter":

> Her uncleanness was in her skirts;
>   she took no thought of her future;
> her downfall was appalling,
>   with none to comfort her. (1:9; see vv. 17, 21)

This is a quite remarkable statement, because in the ideology of exceptionalism, God is always our refuge and strength, a very present help in trouble (Psalm 46:1). But not now! Israel, amid its loss, can continue to ponder the old verities of divine fidelity:

> The steadfast love of the LORD never ceases,
>   his mercies never come to an end;

they are new every morning;
    great is your faithfulness. (Lamentations 3:22-23)

In the end, however, Israel is not so sure, certainly no longer presumptuous about divine fidelity. As the final poem ends, Israel gives voice to the deep complexity of its social reality that is no longer situated in ideological certainty. In quick succession, the poem

- engages in an old-fashioned doxology with its treasured "forever":

  But you, O LORD, reign **forever**;
      your throne endures to all generations. (5:19)

- entertains the thought of divine abandonment:

  Why have you forgotten us completely?
      Why have you forsaken us these many days? (5:20)

- dares to pray in imperatives for new possibility:

  Restore us to yourself, O LORD, that we may be restored;
      renew our days as of old. (5:21)

- finishes with an ambiguous uncertainty:

  unless you have utterly rejected us,
      and are angry with us beyond measure. (5:22)

It is impossible to imagine a more bewildered ending to a poem. The ones left in the abandoned city still knew the cadences of chosenness. But those cadences are no longer fully reliable. Israel has moved to candor about its profound loss. It does not, as of yet, go further. That, however, is already an enormous move away from exceptionalism. It is a move made possible by the anticipation and articulation of grief among the prophets. It is, more than that, made possible by the "keeners," those artists of sadness who refused any cover-up of loss. The cover-up is abandoned both by the deportees in Babylon who "sat and wept" and by those remaining in Jerusalem who were, as they knew, with "no comforter." When the cover-up is broken, it becomes possible to breathe again. In denial, one can only hold one's breath. But now, with sadness inhaled, Israel can live into the emotive world of conflict and estrangement, all honestly voiced in the presence of God and neighbor.

III.

The U.S. political economy, abetted by reassuring religion, rests upon an ideology of exceptionalism that both fosters and requires denial. There can be no doubt that the force of exceptionalism is huge in the self-understanding of U.S. citizens. I write this as I have been watching the Summer Olympics in London. One cannot help but notice that the U.S. spectator-fans, more than any other national group with its own mantra, will readily break out in chants of "USA, USA" in any competition where U.S. athletes may prevail. On the morning I write, August 1, the U.S. women's gymnastic team has just won the gold medal, especially over the Russians. The sports headline in the *New York Times* is "U.S. Flies High and Stands Alone." Of course! With its might and wealth and self-confidence, the U.S. characteristically flies high and stands alone! And of course NBC's singular preoccupation with U.S. victories reaffirms that sense of singularity. There is no better example of the liturgic reinforcement of U.S. exceptionalism than NBC's programming of the Olympics. The denial part is in rarely showing any Chinese victory. There can be no doubt of the deep conviction of U.S. exceptionalism that runs across the spectrum of political opinion. The U.S. is seen to be a peculiar nation state, grounded in freedom that has transcended the old European patterns of public life, a democracy in which social mobility is available, with energy and imagination that are unrivaled anywhere else in the world. Every political leader, moreover, is compelled to be an advocate for such U.S. exceptionalism. Perhaps the political process attracts those who are emotionally committed to that exceptionalism, or perhaps the very process requires any ambitious leader to embrace the claim. And no doubt the outcome of such an affirmation is a combination of personal conviction and public requirement. Either way, it is an essential ingredient of public success.

I have already reviewed the substance and force of U.S. exceptionalism in the previous chapter. Here I need only comment on four dimensions of that ideology that are obvious, but for that no less important.

1. U.S. exceptionalism is expressed as military force and the capacity to leverage international affairs to serve the national interest. We do not much like to think about "American empire." But the truth is that the U.S. Empire has displaced the old European empires in the enforcement of Western domination, notably displacing the French in Vietnam and the British in Afghanistan. That American empire has been under way, surely, since the Monroe Doctrine and the expansionism of President Polk. But its present form is rooted in the ambitions of Theodore Roosevelt and his racist preoccupation with the Pacific.

The evidence of this military passion is evident in the lavish patriotism of many, many, many flags on exhibit, in the singing of our national anthem at every public occasion, in the endless church quarrels about U.S. flags in sanctuaries, and above all, in the unstrained "Pentagon budget" that can only be expanded and never criticized. Thus U.S. "greatness" is readily equated with military capacity.

2. U.S. military domination is no doubt a function of economic domination and the endless flow of wealth to the United States. There is no doubt, moreover, that the U.S. economy has flourished to some great extent through control of international markets and natural resources (oil). In a defining way "globalization" has meant U.S. domination.

The spin-off of that economic domination, in the lives of individual citizens, has been an inordinately high standard of living, the assumption of a continually growing and expanding economy, and a sense of entitlement to the resources and goods of the world for our own benefit. While eschewing the terms of empire, the U.S. has depended upon "colonial" contributions to sustain such privilege and entitlement. The ideological force of such "economic possibility" is evident in the continuing assumption of the underprivileged and disadvantaged that they too can succeed and benefit from such wealth. Thus the disadvantaged are recruited into support of the national interest, not least in a willingness to be cannon fodder in the wars for "American democracy." Benedict Anderson is surely correct that a nation is essentially an act of imagination, and exceptionalism nourishes the imagination of a political process in which all can succeed to prosperity and security.[3]

3. The definers of U.S. exceptionalism, since Governor John Winthrop's "city on a hill," have been northern Europeans. The "political class" until recently has been white Anglo-Saxon Protestants who have encouraged exceptionalism, most especially for those who come from the right places with the right pedigrees and traditions. As a consequence, U.S. exceptionalism comes with a good bit of racism and a sense of the superiority of

3. Benedict Anderson, *Imagined Communities: Reflections on the Origin and Spread of Nationalism* (rev. ed.; New York: Verso, 2006).

73

white Euro-Americans without including the "others," notably African Americans, who are rooted in slave trade, Asian Americans, who have been regarded for too long as the "Yellow Peril," and Hispanic Americans, who are regarded as a threat to jobs for "real Americans." That racist component has been well reviewed by James Bradley in his commentary on the imperial policies of Theodore Roosevelt that came to shameless expression in the internment policies of World War II concerning Japanese-Americans.[4] And, of course, of late the endless agitation that President Obama is not an American is an appeal to racism, with a tacit sense that only "good whites" are "real Americans."

4. A fourth element of exceptionalism is, of course, the religious component. There is no doubt that a sense of national identity as the nearly chosen people of God has propelled much of U.S. self-understanding, and now the religious right, in "defense of the U.S. Constitution," pursues the goal of imposing a certain set of "Christian values" on the public process. That more-or-less theocratic agenda contradicts the elemental idea of welcoming diversity that is at the heart of U.S. exceptionalism, but of course such contradictions are easily overcome in the practice of ideology.

It is the burden of my comments here to indicate the way in which such exceptionalism permits and requires denial of the facts on the ground.

The extravagant commitment to military domination leads to a denial of the reality that the U.S. cannot for long afford to be the single surviving superpower. Our most recent wars — Vietnam, Iraq, and Afghanistan — have exhibited the limits of U.S.

4. James Bradley, *The Imperial Cruise: A Secret History of Empire and War* (New York: Little, Brown, 2009).

military capacity. Beyond that, of course, the rise of Chinese economic-military power — acknowledged by the recent redeployment of U.S. military to the Pacific — means that U.S. domination has important limits that cannot be overcome by louder exceptionalism. The over-sized Pentagon budget that is beyond criticism denies that such military capacity is limited and that economic resources to sustain it cannot be constantly expanded. The maintenance of such a budgetary commitment depends on the denial of limits.[5]

The endlessly expanding U.S. economy — or now the notion of reviving the old U.S. economy — denies economic realities. It is clear that neither political persuasion of government-supported wealth or of free-market deregulation has taken into account the fact that there is no quick fix, no prospect of a comeback to old levels of prosperity. The free transport to capital and the utilization of cheap labor from elsewhere mean that the economy is now managed in ways that have no deep interest in the national good.

The economy, moreover, is skewed to serve a shrinking oligarchy of enormously wealthy persons whose inordinate wealth is matched by the loss of economic viability among a large part of the population.[6] That oligarchy now dominates every facet of public life and is shamelessly greedy, thus is a predatory oligarchy with vulnerable members of society becoming the prey, most often the unwitting prey. It is the mantra of "opportunity"

---

5. Paul Kennedy, *The Rise and Fall of the Great Powers: Economic Change and Military Conflict from 1500 to 2000* (New York: Random House, 1987), has traced the way in which modern empires spend themselves to weakness by military expenditure.

6. On the formation of the U.S. oligarchy, see Jacob S. Hacker and Paul Pierson, *Winner-Take-All Politics: How Washington Made the Rich Richer — and Turned Its Back on the Middle Class* (New York: Simon & Schuster, 2010).

or "freedom" that covers over the insatiable greed of the oligarchy that skews the public process. Thus the U.S. Supreme Court decision concerning *Citizens United v. Federal Election Commission* has allowed greed "opportunity" to run roughshod over the common good. The recent so-called debates over health care policy exhibit the power of concentrated wealth to pretend that a free market solution is on a level playing field in the best interest of the citizens. But it is exactly the illusion of a level playing field that makes current health care policy one of brutalizing triage. The coalition of managed news, deregulation, and courts that are allied with the oligarchy leads to an unworkable public process. But the ideology seduces the vulnerable into imagining that it is other than it is.

The racist component of U.S. exceptionalism features a denial of the actual constitution of the U.S. population. The current rant against "immigrants" has a racist element to it in which there is, among the ideologues, a sense of being overwhelmed by those who are not "real Americans." The efforts to sustain the old patterns of racist domination fly in the face of democratic commitments. Indeed, much of the resistance to "big government" and to trade unions is the passion of an old white citizenry to be sure that others do not have access to the common wealth that is among us.

It hardly needs to be said that the religious component of this ideology of exceptionalism has to deny that Christian faith in any responsible form is a practice of neighborly hospitality, generosity, and inclusiveness. But the force of the ideology can skew even gospel claims to the contrary.

This combination of military illusion, economic distortion, racist posturing, and skewed religion amounts to an effort to sustain a practice of denial. The purpose of the denial, I suggest, is to maintain old privilege and entitlement and to fend off the reality of the world. The practical consequence is that we have a society that in truth is not working for a large number of people.[7] The "not working" is indicated by all kinds of social indices about health, education, jobs, and housing. The "not working" is helped along by the tacit appeal to violence as a way to order society, all the way from an exploitative prison system, to "Stand Your Ground" laws, to agribusiness that diminished the land for the sake of profit, to the unrestrained gun lobby, to acceptance of torture as a viable government procedure. The sum of these practices is unbearable to the body politic. But they are made "acceptable" through appeals to the ideology of exceptionalism that gives warrant for the distortion of social reality.

The practice of such ideology depends, moreover, on the cunning use of euphemisms, so that things are not called by their right names (see Isaiah 5:20). Every violent regime, including ours, has to resort to euphemisms to cover over the reality of practice. The Reverend Billy can say of our practice of distorted language:

> We can't believe that bomb is called security.
> We can't believe that monopoly is called democracy.
> We can't believe that gasoline prices are called
> foreign policy . . .
> We can't believe that racism is called crime fighting!
> We can't believe that sweatshops are called efficiency!
> We can't believe that a mall is called the neighborhood! . . .
> We can't believe that advertising is called free speech!
> We can't believe that love is called for sale!

7. See Timothy Noah, *The Great Divergence: America's Growing Inequality Crisis and What We Can Do about It* (New York: Bloomsbury, 2012).

We can't believe that you think there are two political parties!
We can't believe that you repeat the word "democracy"
   like it's liturgical chant from a lost religion![8]

The occurrence of 9/11 is a pivot point in the history of U.S. exceptionalism, as was the destruction of Jerusalem in ancient Israel. That event, fed by hostility toward the "American empire," exhibited the extreme vulnerability of the U.S.:

It suggested that military security could not protect us. Witness the frantic efforts of Homeland Security.

It suggested that the concentration of wealth in the U.S. was not sufficient to guarantee privilege in the world.

It demonstrated resentment toward the U.S.'s largely unexamined way in the world.

It suggested that God is not unqualifiedly "on our side."

Of course our characteristic national response was to settle even more passionately on our exceptionalism, to explain away the hostility because of our "love of freedom." Even that, I propose, was an act of denial, for such an explanation refused to think about the military, economic, and racist elements of practice that would evoke such vigorous resentment.

The action of 9/11 could have led us to review and reconsider the claims of exceptionalism and to come to a fresh appreciation of the alternative dimensions of exceptionalism as a "city on a hill." But it did not! It did not because the response itself was yet another step in denial. The passionate appeal to exceptionalism sounds hauntingly like the verdict of Jeremiah on his ancient society (6:13-15; 8:10-12):

8. Bill Talen, *What Should I Do if Reverend Billy Is in My Store?* (New York: New Press, 2003), 93-94.

Everyone is greedy for unjust gain;
They say "Peace, peace" when there is no peace;
They do not know how to blush.

It is an open question whether there is yet an elemental "therefore" to follow as in 6:15; 8:12.

The ideology precludes any notion of such an ominous "therefore." We go on, not unlike Jerusalem, imagining a prompt return to a lost normalcy.

IV.

The prophetic task, amid a culture of denial, is to embrace, model, and practice grief, in order that the real losses in our lives can be acknowledged. The purpose of such a performance of sadness is so the things we deeply treasure among us and have lost may be fully relinquished.

There is indeed enough loss among us to evoke profound sadness, just as there was in ancient Jerusalem. That sadness at loss, moreover, is widely felt at deep levels of our life; but felt loss and sadness contradict the ideology of exceptionalism and the required denial. For all of our readiness to deny, our sense of loss persists:

- We are at the edge of having lost our political-military hegemony in the world. The failure of recent military adventures and the preoccupation with Chinese power attest to a loss of confidence. And all the strutting buoyancy of patriotic mantras cannot hide that loss.
- We have lost much of our economic leverage in the world. This is evident when U.S. leaders can no longer dominate the meetings of G8 and the other configurations of global eco-

nomic power. Indeed, the U.S. economy is to some extent at the mercy of the management of the Euro. That inevitable interdependence of economies of course tells powerfully against U.S. domination.

The waning of global economic influence, for the most part, does not directly impact most of us. But the impact of that waning is strongly felt in the slowdown of our economy, the loss of economic benefits, and the difficulty of maintaining a high standard of living on an income that fails to keep pace with the cost of a "good living." And, of course, diminished income leads to a lesser collection of tax dollars and thus the shrinking of public institutions. The passion for privatization is only the illusion that those with resources can maintain a "separate peace" apart from the failed public economy.

- We, a certain "we," have lost the capacity to maintain "our kind of America" that is populated solely by white neighbors, led by males, limited to heterosexuals. That profile of "proper American" continues to have great persuasive power, but of course demographics on all counts tell against it. It turns out that the radical diversification of ethnic origins among us, the full emergence of women's power, and the willing outing of gays contradict that old wish world of "America." Thus the current campaign contending that President Obama is not a real American or does not understand how America works is a mix of anxiety about loss and a racist wish for the recovery of a world that is gone.
- We in old-line churches are experiencing an institutional free fall in numbers, dollars, and missional energy. Of course the "blame game" goes on apace, that the loss is because of being "too liberal" or some such. But in fact the loss is complex and not readily explained.

- This converging loss that is beyond denial, concerning loss of political-military hegemony, loss of economic dominance, loss of social-ethnic singularity, and loss of ecclesiastical prosperity, has come to amount to a loss of moral certainty and a failure of nerve about the future. In sum, we watch as the world for which we had prepared ourselves and had learned to master is disappearing before our very eyes.

That loss that touches every dimension of our common life is too painful to acknowledge. It can only be talked about around the edges, because the characteristic tone of public discourse among us is, perforce, upbeat, buoyant, and optimistic. Our political leaders are required to promise a recovery and a return to normalcy. Our moral teachers are expected to "get the train back on track." Our military leaders are expected to promise that one more "surge" of troops or one more budget expansion at the Pentagon will assure continued hegemony. Religious gurus are appreciated for offering "six steps" to a vibrant church or any other quick fix. We are, by an ideology of exceptionalism, on every front mandated to entertain a return to well-being, dominance, hegemony. For that reason every U.S. medal at the Olympics is taken as another sign of recovered greatness, and every political leader must recite the casual petition "God bless America" — God bless "America more than any other." In such an ideological cocoon, we are scandalized by Jeremiah Wright, in his daring truth-telling, who can say out loud, "God damn America," while failing to notice that he was only asserting that "what we sow we reap."

The sadness at loss remains unvoiced and silent. For that reason, sadness at loss must come to expression in less direct ways. It comes to expression in ways of anxiety, albeit inchoate and inarticulate, that yield in practice parsimony, inhospitality, and vengefulness, all in the service of a would-be return to normalcy. Thus I believe that the "Tea Party" enterprise is a measure of the wish to have our old world back again. "Stand Your Ground" laws attempt to legitimate violence in the maintenance of an old order against those who contradict that old order. I have no doubt, moreover, that the lavish adrenalin expended against gays and lesbians is, in the first instance, not about gays and lesbians. It is rather a desperate wish for an old world order that is more comfortable and reassuring. Thus on all fronts there is a kind of vigorous, shameless nostalgia among us for a world that is gone and will not be recovered:

- U.S. military hegemony is gone!
- U.S. economic domination is gone!
- Preferred racial-ethnic singularity is gone!
- Simplistic moral certitudes are gone!

Anyone who has long benefitted from these old arrangements (including this writer) has much reason for sadness!

But set this down: sadness over loss that is unvoiced, unembraced, and unacknowledged a) turns to violence and b) precludes movement toward new possibility. Sadness unvoiced leads to violence, whether expressed in racial bigotry, hostility toward outsiders, readiness for attack on enemies, or self-hatred. Sadness unvoiced leads to a backward wish for recovery; as a result no energy is left for the pursuit or practice of new social possibility that lies beyond our old comfort zones. Thus our public discourse is largely cast as a yearning for the way it used to be, with old-time privilege and old-time religion cast in comfortable country music that requires nothing.

Given that state of legitimate sadness that is kept numb and unvoiced, the prophetic task, I propose, is to encourage, permit, and engage the practice of public grief over a world that is gone. This is, I have shown, what the prophets did as they anticipated the coming destruction. This is what they did as they cast YHWH as the chief mourner (keener) over Jerusalem that was taken from them via the God-presided vagaries of history. And that is surely what is being done in these negating communal songs of grief that boldly contradict the "Songs of Zion" (Psalms 74, 79, 137) that ponder the demise of city, king, and temple. That practice, moreover, came to fullest expression in the book of Lamentations. These poems of grief that stopped well short of restoration were on the lips of those "left behind" in Jerusalem, so that they had every day to see the ruined walls and to smell the smoldering, still smoking residue of the city in shambles.

Such voiced grief — in anticipation, on the lips of YHWH, and in the wake of loss — enacted the painful process of relinquishment. The task in death is to let go of what is finished, dead, and failed. The ideology of exceptionalism, with its favorite modifier "forever," insisted that such an ending could not come. For that reason, every sign of such an ending must be denied. But the assurance of "forever" and the required denial do not and cannot cancel the facts on the ground or dispose of the sense of free fall that persists in spite of willed denial.

The alternative toward health and new life is the shared, out loud, honest work of grief. Such voiced grief is an alternative to violence. Such grief, moreover, turns loss to energy for newness. Thus it is, I propose, the very voicing of loss that permitted displaced and dislocated Jews to do the work of articulating covenantal faith in quite different and venturesome categories after the loss of Jerusalem.

Thus I propose that the prophetic community, right in the middle of a culture of denial, is a proper venue for grief work. Such a meeting will not, at the outset, be "the happiest place in town." It will only be the most honest place in town, where honesty is not an extreme concern in a culture of denial.

I can think of three beginning points for such public work of grief:

1. The recovery of the psalms of lament is an urgent pastoral task. It is simply astonishing that in its attachment to an alliance with dominant culture the church has avoided the lament psalms (with the notable unavoidable exception of Psalm 22 that is on the lips of Jesus). And even where we may occasionally use such a psalm, the "hard verses" are omitted from the lectionary and censored from use.

Indeed, at the London Olympics a six-minute segment of the wondrous opening ceremony was omitted by NBC in its U.S.A. coverage. That segment was a memorial for recent victims of violence that concluded with the singing of "Abide with Me." NBC said that coverage was "tailored for our American audience." I assume such an audience, not accustomed to hearing laments even in church, must be protected from death and from songs of trust in the midst of death. But Israel, amid the loss of Jerusalem, knew better. The laments tell the truth about the city and about God who is capable of abandoning failed chosenness.

2. We may pay attention to the rich legacy of contemporary laments that grieve over the failure of our "system" of well-being. Such laments arise among the excluded, powerless, and vulnerable — not the kind of people who constitute usual church voices. But these voices provide a script that we are able to echo, because such voices match and give freedom to our sadness. As exemplars of such laments, consider the following.

How Much Faith?

So how much faith do we possess?
From where does our financial security come?
The economic crisis has deeply touched
both our emotional and spiritual lives
and we are compelled to ask deep questions.
If our lifestyles are radically altered; that is,

If our houses, cars and most of our possessions are lost
and our savings and retirement accounts become depleted
and we can no longer afford health coverage,
in what fashion will we then pray
and what will be the nature of our worship,
our praise and our thanksgiving to God?
Might all those turn to laments,
the kind of laments that the vast majority
of people throughout the world
have voiced for centuries?
They knew the grinding lifestyle of poverty
long before the sin of avarice gave birth
to our own present crisis.[9]

After Katrina

There's no Sabbath in this house.
Just work.
The black of garbage bags,
yellow-cinched throats opening
to gloved hands.
Black tombs along the road now,
proof she knew to cherish
the passing things,
even those muted before the waters came
before the mold's grotesquerie
and the wooden house choked on bones.
My aunt wades through the wreckage, failing,
no matter how hard she tries,
at letting go.

---

9. Al Staggs, "How Much Faith?" in *In Mammon We Trust* (Cleveland, TN: Parson's Porch, 2011), 13.

I look on, glad, at her failing,
her slow rites
fingering what she'd once been given to care for.
The waistbands of her husband's briefs,
elastic as memory;
the blank stare of rotted drawers,
their irises of folded linen still,
smelling of soap and wood
and clean hands.
Daylight through the silent soft windows
And I'm sure now: Today is Sabbath,
the work we do, prayer.
I know what she releases into the garbage bags,
shiny like the wet skins of seals,
beached on the shore of this house.[10]

We Cry Out

We cry out for what we have lost, and we remember you
again. We look for each other, we cannot find us, and we remember you. From the ground of no purpose our children
accuse us, and we remember, we recall a purpose. Could it
be? we wonder. And here is death. Could it possibly be? And
here is old age. And we never knew; we never stood up, and
the good land was taken from us, and the sweet family was
crushed. Maybe, we said, it could be, and we gave it a place
among the possibilities. I'll do it myself, we said, as shame
thickened the faculties of the heart. And the first reports
were of failure, and the second of mutilations, and the third
of every abomination. We remember, we cry out to you to

10. Kevin Simmonds, "After Katrina," in *After Shocks: The Poetry of Recovery for Life-Shattering Events*, ed. Tom Lombardo (Atlanta: Sante Lucia, 2008), 290-91.

return our soul. Is it really upon us? Yes, it is upon us. Do we merit this? Yes, we merit this. We cry out for what we have lost, and we remember you. We remember the containing word, the holy channels of commandment, and goodness waiting forever on the Path. And here and there, among the seventy tongues and the hundred darknesses — something, something shining, men of courage strengthening themselves to kindle the lights of repentance.[11]

Never Say
Never say you've come to the end of the way,
Though leaden skies blot out the light of the day.
The hour we all long for will surely appear —
Our steps will thunder with the words: We are here!
From lands of palm trees to far-off lands of snow,
We come with anguish, we come with grief, with pain
    and woe;
And where our blood flowed right before our eyes,
There our power'll bloom, our courage will arise.
The glow of morning sun will gild a bright today,
Night's darkness vanish, like the enemy cast away.
But if we perish before this dawn's begun —
This song's a message passed to daughter and to son.
In blood this song was written, and not with pen or quill,
Not from a songbird freely flying as he will.
Sung by a people crushed by falling walls —
Sung with guns in hand, by those whom freedom calls![12]

11. Leonard Cohen, "We Cry Out," in *Stranger Music: Selected Poems and Songs* (New York: Pantheon, 1993), 327.

12. Hirsh Glik, "Never Say," in *Truth and Lamentation: Stories and Poems on the Holocaust*, ed. Milton Teichman and Sharon Leder (Urbana: University of Illinois Press, 1994), 249.

3. But after biblical laments and remembered poems of pain and loss attention must be paid to the laments of truth voiced by those close at hand. Every pastor knows such voices of bewilderment and pain and rage and loss. We treat such voices "therapeutically," as we should. We may, however, also take them as serious acts of relinquishment when they are well received and attentively honored. Pain does yearn to speak! And be heard! We all too often fail to attend to such pain, it being denied in an ocean of exceptionalism.

The work of relinquishment is hard done. It must be done! There is no shortcut. The task requires trust that does not blush and history that does not blink. It is as though, embracing our loss, we offer a requiem for a lost world, willing to let it rest in the embrace of honest words. It is thought by many interpreters that the laments in the book of Psalms regularly and characteristically evoked a salvation oracle in response: "Do not fear" (see Isaiah 41:10, 13, 14; 43:1, 5; 44:8). Do not fear to tell the truth. Do not fear to relinquish. That phrase, "do not fear," is more than a response to lament. It is an indispensable premise for such relinquishing lament. Prophetic ministry is courage for such fearlessness, even in a culture that endlessly reminds us "Be very afraid." Be afraid of relinquishing this failed world, because there is no other. Honest lament knows better. It knows that relinquishment positions us to receive . . . yet again.

IV

Hope amid Despair

Accept no mitigation
but be instructed at the null point:
the zero
breeds new algebra.

AMOS WILDER

When the destruction of Jerusalem was fully processed and had sunk in, the texture of Israel's faith was abruptly and profoundly changed — emotionally, politically, and theologically.

- Emotionally, Israel arrived at a deep sense of loss, so deep that the denial provided by an ideology of exceptionalism was broken open. Consequently, Israel could genuinely experience the loss, as is evident in the laments I have already cited.
- Politically, the end of the Jerusalem establishment as a source of power was now acknowledged. There would be no "next king." The temple was empty! Israel now had to live on terms other than its own, on the terms of the Babylonian superpower that gave no credence to the "local traditions" of Israel.
- Theologically, Israel had now to struggle with evidence that YHWH no longer honored the chosenness of Jerusalem, king, temple, or city. The erstwhile deep confidence, expressed li-

turgically, ensuring chosenness and YHWH's attentive fidelity to Israel was now evidently in great question.

The scene shifts from an emotional sense of well-being to one of **loss**, from a political sense of guarantee to one of acute **vulnerability**, from a theological sense of chosenness to one of **abandonment**. That new context of loss, vulnerability, and abandonment amounted to a vindication of prophetic realism against the ideology of exceptionalism and of prophetic grief against denial. Now the scene shifts to a new generation, the ones who were either "left behind" and impotent in Jerusalem or the ones deported to the waters of Babylon to ponder, in weeping, their new situation. Now there was no more ground for trusting and affirming the ancient ideology of exceptionalism and no more reason to practice the denial that had seemed both necessary and viable. The new context for faith was one of emotional, political, and theological free fall without a discernible bottom. I propose that 9/11 has had, acknowledging the different contexts, the same impact on our society, emotional, politically, and theologically. That sense of free fall is evident, I propose, in the powerful, even if amorphous, anxiety that now marks every dimension of our common life.

I.

The generation of Israelites who lived through and looked back on the destruction of Jerusalem drew very close to despair. How could they not! The destruction of the city and the deportation of the king visibly negated all of the certitudes upon which they had counted.

The major population was left behind in the ruins of the city. It is common among us to conclude that the book of Lamentations voices the anguished loss of those who remained in the city. They were subject, every day, to the sights and smells of a city in shambles. Thus the poems of Lamentations describe in imaginative detail the deep sense of abandonment made evident in the ruins. It was that population that could conclude:

> My soul is bereft of peace;
>> I have forgotten what happiness is;
> so I say, "Gone is my glory,
>> and all that I had hoped for from the LORD."
>
> (Lamentations 3:17-18)

Gone! The Hebrew term, 'abad, means "perish." It has all been destroyed. Gone is the city, gone is the king, gone is the temple, gone is a sense of chosenness, gone is the guarantee of protection, gone is the assumption of entitled specialness. What else could be concluded from the evidence? The lines continue with bitterness and abasement:

> The thought of my affliction and my homelessness
>> is wormwood and gall!
> My soul continually thinks of it
>> and is bowed down within me. (vv. 19-20)

The term rendered in NRSV as "homelessness" likely means "trouble." The translation "homelessness" appeals to Isaiah 58:7, which speaks of the acutely needy. While the term is elusive, it parallels "affliction" and describes a context of deep, vulnerable need.

To be sure, the makers of this poem rally in verses 21-24 with the three great terms for divine fidelity: steadfast love, mercies, faithfulness. That recall permits a better conclusion:

> Therefore I have hope. (v. 21)

It is, however, a hope that is not well sustained in the poetry that follows. The poetry of Lamentations ends close to abject despair. By the end in 5:22, it is clear that Israel does not know and cannot be any longer certain of YHWH's continued fidelity. All of the old assurances are now in deep dispute.

The population that was deported to Babylon is commonly thought to be different from those "left behind." That population is not large. According to Jeremiah 52:28-30, it amounted to only 4,600 persons. That population, moreover, was elite and connected enough to make its own way in a new circumstance. In critical interpretation, moreover, this community is plausibly to be situated amid the buoyant poetry of Isaiah 40-55 with all of its positive prospects. Indeed, Isaiah 40-55 is often thought to be as "answer" to the laments of the book of Lamentations.[1] Thus as Lamentations declares "None to comfort" (1:2), so this Isaiah poetry begins "Comfort, O comfort" (40:1). If we rightly locate Lamentations in Jerusalem and Isaiah 40-55 in Babylon, then the faith of the deported community answers the disconsolation of the community left behind. And indeed, it is the community of the deported that eventually issues in the initiatives of Ezra and Nehemiah and the recharacterization of Israel that became Judaism.

But the distinctions of

- left behind . . . deported,
- Lamentations . . . Isaiah 40–55,
- disconsolation . . . hope

are not as clear as all of that. The reason that one is not so easily contrasted with the other is that we can see that the lamenting

---

1. See Patricia Tull Willey, *Remember the Former Things: The Recollection of Previous Texts in Second Isaiah* (Society of Biblical Literature Dissertation Series 161; Atlanta: Scholars, 1997).

near-despair of the Jerusalem community (in the book of Lamentations) was known and practiced in the community of the deportees as well. After all, the two communities were not hermetically sealed off from each other, but were in close contact. The elites were not immune to the near-despair of the Jerusalem survivors. What transpired in the liturgies of the survivors in Jerusalem would have been known and in some instances appropriated for use in the deported community. We may cite three uses that show that the near-despair of the community in Jerusalem was taken up as the practice of lament in the Babylonian community of Jews. Both communities voiced their near-despair.

1. In Isaiah 40:27, the poet who will voice hope in Babylon quotes Israel as posing a question:

> Why do you say, O Jacob,
>   and speak, O Israel . . . ?

The question is a reprimand, suggesting, from the perspective of the poet, that such complaint is inappropriate. But the poet nonetheless quotes the complaint that must have been current among the deportees:

> My way is hidden from the LORD,
>   and my right is disregarded by my God.

The complaint here attributed to these displaced persons is an accusation against YHWH. The poet charges the deportees are making accusation against YHWH. This attributed liturgic assertion is the claim that YHWH does not notice the situation of Israel, that YHWH is indifferent to "my justice." The implication is that Israel, in its displacement, deserves better than that from YHWH and issues a protest against YHWH on the basis of its old entitlement. Thus the displacement of the sixth century is treated in the complaint as evidence that YHWH has reneged on the old fidelity to which YHWH is pledged and upon which Israel has counted. This complaint is echoed in the protesting wonderment of Psalm 89, voiced in the Psalm after many verses of affirmation of divine fidelity:

> Lord, where is your steadfast love of old,
> which by your faithfulness you swore to David? (v. 49)

Historical experience leads to a conclusion of YHWH's disregard and nullification of old promised faithfulness.

2. In Isaiah 49:14, the poet again quotes Israel, with "Zion said." No doubt the quotation is from liturgical usage:

> The LORD has forsaken me,
> my Lord has forgotten me.

The parallel lines feature the word pair "forsake, forget." Indeed, this same poet in 54:7 can have YHWH admit the momentary "forsaking" (the same word rendered in NRSV as "abandoned"). The reference to "hide my face" in 54:8 is clearly reminiscent of the accusation against YHWH in 40:27.

The double use of "forsake, forget" would seem to be a direct quotation from the lament of Lamentations 5:20:

> Why have you forgotten us completely?
> Why have you forsaken us these many days?

In this lament the verbs are underscored by the modifiers "completely" and "many days," suggesting that divine abandonment is for perpetuity. There can be no doubt that the poet in Babylon had heard his company reciting the laments practiced in Jerusalem. Thus the surviving community, in both venues, is preoccupied with divine default. We may notice, moreover, that in Isaiah 49:14, the statement is a simple indicative; in Lamentations, with the "why," it is more likely a reprimand. In both cases the community struggles with the awareness of divine abandonment, neglect, and absence.

3. The third evidence of lament of near-despair is given not in the quoted voice of Israel, as in 40:27 and 49:14. It is given, rather, in a divine response to an implied accusation. In Isaiah 50:2, the divine response is in a double rhetorical question:

Is my hand shortened, that it cannot redeem?
    Or have I no power to deliver?

The two questions imply and respond to an accusation that YHWH has no capacity to save Israel. In context that double question, reinforced by an absolute infinitive for "shortened," must have grown out of a complaint of Israel that judged that YHWH had no power to save. That would be a judgment made on the basis of loss and displacement. That is, if YHWH had such power, there would not have been displacement. Since it did happen, the only "reasonable" conclusion is that YHWH was not strong enough to defend Israel. Here it is to be noted that it is a question of divine power, not divine fidelity or resolve. That verdict of divine impotence attributed to Israel is vigorously answered and refuted in the next lines:

By my rebuke I dry up the sea,
    I make the rivers a desert;
their fish stink for lack of water,
    and die of thirst.

I clothe the heavens with blackness,
and make sackcloth their covering. (Isaiah 50:2-3)

In the typical scope of this Isaiah poetry, the answer is in the huge vista of creation.

The same theme is treated, again as divine response to alleged complaint, in Isaiah 59:1:

See, the LORD's hand is not too short to save,
nor his ear too dull to hear. (59:1)

Here the statement is a simple indicative, but the question has lingered after chapter 50. The notion of divine default is not easily disposed of.

These three complaints in 40:27; 49:14; and 50:2 (on which see also 59:1), suggest that complaint was vigorous in both communities of survivors and that the complaint was significant enough that it required a response on behalf of YHWH. In the large scheme of Israel's faith, it cannot be said that Israel finally ended in despair. Or if there were those who ended in despair, they have disappeared from the narrative life of the Old Testament. But we should not settle too readily for the "canonical" assurance that despair was not given definitive voice in the tradition.

Whatever may be the final word of the tradition, along the way Israel dares to go deeply into despair. Perhaps the saving element is that such a propensity to despair, required by visible, experienced circumstance, is kept in engaged conversation, for such engaged conversation is finally the antidote to despair. It is not so easy, however, to assure the successful management of despair, and the despair must be given its due, a due commensurate with the facts on the ground.

In his remarkable book weighing the claims of Sigmund Freud and William James, Richard Beck considers Freud's claim that religion is simply an illusion that offers consolation. Critiquing that reductionist claim that continues to dominate much secular thought, Beck considers James's distinction between the "healthy soul" and the "sick soul." But James's labels require careful attention, else we might conclude that the "sick soul" is deficient and weak in contrast to the "healthy soul," a judgment that James surely did not intend. Beck shows from James's analysis that such a "sick soul" is theologically serious, does not seek easy consolation, and is able to go deeply and honestly into the darkness of divine failure and infidelity. Beck's argument serves to refute Freud's notion of illusion for consolation by showing that such religiously serious persons do not seek and do not find consolation in their faith. Rather, they find realism about their circumstance in which they linger with courage and in which they practice their faith in God. Thus Beck concludes:

> In the face of a suffering and broken world, belief in divine solicitousness and special protection is hard to come by for sick souls. In fact, just the opposite seems to be the case; God is decidedly *unhelpful* and, rather than providing protection, is allowing suffering to continue, often in ways that leave us trembling in sadness, shock, despair, and horror.
>
> These experiences are difficult to face. They infuse life with a sense of existential despair. Even though it might be easier, simply as a matter of coping, to hide our eyes from life (as many do), the sick souls refuse to look away. They refuse the too easy retreat into existentially consoling beliefs. And the price they pay for this is allowing a painful tension to sit at the center of their existence, a belief in a God who is often not present and who often fails to rescue.[2]

2. Richard Beck, *The Authenticity of Faith: The Varieties and Illusions of Religious Experience* (Abilene: Abilene Christian University Press, 2012), 226-27.

The implication of Beck on James is that serious practitioners of faith do not flinch from despair or seek easy consolations:

> Less motivated by needs for comfort or solace, sick souls should be more willing to tolerate the existentially difficult implications of their faith. Sick souls should be more, rather than less, willing to attribute suffering *to* God, follow Isaiah 45 and hold God responsible for the whole of life. The result is the experience of monotheistic lament we find in the Psalms of lament . . . this is an experience filled with theological tension and cognitive dissonance. Consequently, there is emotional and psychological discomfort. The healthy-minded, according to James, will seek to exit this space as quickly as possible, usually by cracking the faith experience. However, sick souls, being less motivated by a need for comfort, are more likely to linger in this space, perhaps spending their entire lives within this experience. Sick souls would accomplish this by remaining rugged monotheists, refusing to crack God. Sick souls will try to shoulder the full emotional burden of monotheism.[3]

This, I submit, is exactly what is found in the exilic laments of Israel, the haunting, wonder, and courage to go deep into the reality of divine infidelity and disregard. In its lament Israel dares to go to the null point of despair and linger in the abyss of abandonment.

In its usual practice, the church, with its unwitting preference for James's "healthy souls," does not want to go there. Consequently, it does not want to entertain the reality that our ancient ancestors in displacement also did not want to go. Unlike these ancient ancestors in faith, the contemporary church prefers

3. Beck, *The Authenticity of Faith*, 231.

James's "healthy souls" who want to live bravely "without consolation." Thus the church avoids laments. When it reads the book of Lamentations, moreover, it lingers longest over the small affirmation of 3:20-22, and when it reads Isaiah 40–55 (along with Handel), it does not recognize that this is a response to a long series of mantras of "none to comfort."

Beck describes healthy souls as those who are "feeling queasy about the incarnation" and so flee to easier assurances of a gnostic type, hold to a "higher Christology" that skimps on the embodiment of Jesus, and hold a religion of solace that is without darkness.[4] To that extent, Freud is right about religion. But Beck's research shows that Freud's reductionism simply disregards the "saints of darkness" who seek no such easy consolation and who are resolved to face the evident reality of loss, abandonment, and absence.

This is indeed exactly what we find in the laments I have cited. These are faithful voices who refuse any easy consolation. In a neat syllogism, Beck characterizes "winter faith experience" among those who engage in "high communion" and "high complaint." His three other members of the quadrangle are

- *religious critics* who are long on complaint and low on communion,
- *disengaged believers* who are low on complaint and low on communion, and
- *summer faith experience,* healthy minded who are high on communion and low on complaint.[5]

It is clear that the matrix of exile and the interface of Lamentations and Isaiah 40–55 welcome the "winter believers" who

4. Beck, *The Authenticity of Faith*, 197-209.
5. Beck, *The Authenticity of Faith*, 145.

commune intensely with God in God's absence and who practice daring complaint with imaginative daring.

In artistic form, this is the voice of Job:

> Oh, that I had the indictment written by my adversary!
> Surely I would carry it on my shoulder;
>   I would bind it on me like a crown;
> I would give him an account of all my steps;
>   like a prince I would approach him. (Job 31:35-37)

In prophetic tradition, this is the voice of Jeremiah:

> O LORD, you have enticed me,
>   and I was enticed;
> you have overpowered me,
>   and you have prevailed. (Jeremiah 20:7)

Both Jeremiah and Job after him probed the truth of despair. But the text makes clear that such a probe was not limited to exotic, gifted individuals. It was the work of the entire community. It was the truth required by circumstance. It was the truth with which YHWH had to deal. It was the truth that was in touch with everyday reality, that did not deny, that did not cover up, and that did not flinch.

- In ancient Israel, it was painful truth that waited impatiently.
- In Christian tradition, it is the truth of a very long Saturday.[6]
- In our wake of 9/11, it is a script for the saints of darkness who are inescapable carriers of the new algebra that arises at the zero hour.

---

6. See Alan E. Lewis, *Between Cross and Resurrection: A Theology of Holy Saturday* (Grand Rapids: Eerdmans, 2001).

II.

**The prophetic task, in the midst of exilic despair over de-
struction and displacement, is to declare and enact hope for
a buoyant future that is securely in the purview of God.** The
sixth-century displacement, whether remaining in Jerusalem or
lingering "by the waters of Babylon," was indeed the "zero hour"
for Israelites. In that hour no one would have expected the "new
algebra" that came in prophetic declarations of hope. Indeed, the
eruption of prophetic oracles of hope in the midst of the sixth century is among the more remarkable, inexplicable features of the
Old Testament. These oracles of promise, while informed by old
traditions, are not derived from anything past. They purport to
be completely new acts of utterance, underived, given only by the
new resolve of YHWH. That eruption of utterances of hope is said
to be commensurate with the eruption of YHWH's new resolve:

> For a long time I have held my peace,
> I have kept still and restrained myself;
> now I will cry out like a woman in labor,
> I will gasp and pant.
> I will lay waste mountains and hills,
> and dry up all their herbage;
> I will turn the rivers into islands,
> and dry up the pools.
> I will lead the blind
> by a road they do not know,
> by paths that they have not known
> I will guide them.
> I will turn the darkness before them into light,
> the rough places into level ground.
> These are the things I will do,
> and I will not forsake them. (Isaiah 42:14-16)

When "the cry of the heart" is voiced by "the saints of darkness" (à la Richard Beck), no one knows if there will be an answer. One cries out in protest, lament, and complaint, because the silence cannot be maintained (see Psalm 39:1-3). Thus in Exodus 2:23, when the Israelites "groaned under their slavery, and cried out," they did not address anyone, nor did they anticipate an answer. But they nonetheless received one (vv. 24-25). So it is with the complaints I have identified as "voices of despair" in the tradition of Isaiah. They are cries of the heart that do not anticipate response; and yet they receive divine answers of resolve, assurance, and promise.

- The complaint in Isaiah 40:27 receives a divine answer that opens the way for the promissory utterances that follow. The response begins in verses 27-28 with three questions that amount to a reprimand for Israel's doubt and despair:

Why do you say?
Have you not known?
Have you not heard?

You should have known and heard! And if you had known and heard, you would not say . . . Then follows an utterance of what they should have known and heard in exilic Israel, namely, a doxology to YHWH the creator. It is credible to think that Israel in its displacement had long since given up such doxological claims, both because of despair and because of Babylonian coercive dismissal of the claims of YHWH. Nonetheless, doxology to YHWH erupts exactly amid the despair:

The LORD is the everlasting God,
    the Creator of the ends of the earth.
He does not faint or grow weary,

his understanding is unsearchable.
He gives power to the faint,
   and strength to the powerless. (vv. 28-29)

The outcome of that reality of *power* to the faint and *strength* to the powerless, stated in verses 30-31, is a newly energized community:

Even youths will faint and be weary,
   and the young will fall exhausted;
but those who wait for the LORD shall renew their strength,
   they shall mount up with wings like eagles,
they shall run and not be weary,
   they shall walk and not faint.

The reality of YHWH, uttered in hope that contradicts despair, concerns mounting up (soaring), running, walking, no more weariness and fainting. The Babylonian Empire no doubt preferred Jews who languished in despair, who had no energy to run, no stamina to walk, no courage to soar, and thus no threat to the empire. All of that, however, is contradicted by the utterance of hope that brings YHWH back into play. The pivot of the oracle is the term "wait," that is, hope, the refusal to accept or conform to the closed world of imperial reduction. The utterance mediates a transformed reality that the empire-induced despair had nullified. Given prophetic utterance, that transforming reality of YHWH, the creator, refuses to remain nullified.

- The lament in Isaiah 49:14, a quotation from the book of Lamentations, is answered in the oracle of verses 15-18. As in 40:27-28, the response begins with a rhetorical question (v. 15). The wonderment is whether a nursing mother can forget her child. The expected answer is "No, she cannot forget." But the poet surprises by answering, "Yes, she might forget." But then, with a disjunctive "yet," the reality of YHWH is contrasted with a nursing mother who might indeed forget. Thus the imagery is handled negatively. We expected that YHWH would be like a nursing mother who remembers. But no; YHWH is unlike a nursing mother who might forget. It is the contrast between such human fickleness (where we least expected it) and divine fidelity that is the basis for what follows. The attention getter, "behold" (NRSV "see"), introduces the affirmations that follow. YHWH has written down the name of Israel. The mother *may forget; I will not forget!*

As a consequence the "builders" of Jerusalem, designated by YHWH, will teem to the broken city. Building authorized by YHWH will override the destruction authorized by Babylon. The builders are all around. They "gather" like returnees and will be ornaments of beauty, pride, and delight. The city "turns the corner" from destruction to restoration, authorized by YHWH. This imagery becomes the entry point for the rich poetry of restoration in Isaiah 60-62:

> You shall no more be termed Forsaken,
>   and your land shall no more be termed Desolate;
> but you shall be called My Delight Is in Her,
>   and your land Married;
> for the LORD delights in you,
>   and your land shall be married. . . .
> Go through, go through the gates,
>   prepare the way for the people;
> build up, build up the highway,
>   clear it of stones,
>   lift up an ensign over the peoples. (Isaiah 62:4, 10)

It is no wonder that in the wake of this assurance of divine re-membering, the church can reiterate from God:

> . . . That soul, though all hell should endeavor to shake,
> I'll never, no, never, no, never forsake.[7]

While the lyric spiritualizes and privatizes the resolve of YHWH, the words echo the assurance of the God who never forgets.

- The complaint in Isaiah 50:2 is stated in a rebuking question about a "short hand" with "no power." The answer is already implied in the way the question is posed, but then is given full expression in verses 2-3. The question of a "short hand" for YHWH has been in purview since the wilderness sojourn when there did not seem to be adequate provision for survival. In Numbers 11:22, Moses twice asks, "Are there enough . . . ?" YHWH answers in indignation, both scolding Moses for his doubt and assuring that YHWH is fully capable of giving all that is needed:

> Is the LORD's power limited? Now you shall see whether my word will come true for you or not. (v. 23)

And of course in that narrative, food is given. Now the poet Isaiah picks up the old question and reiterates the old answer. As the question persists in every circumstance of "shortage," so the divine reassurance is uttered in every such circumstance. YHWH characteristically specializes in an "outstretched hand," one that is long enough to reach effectively into every trouble. It is that outstretched hand that performed the exodus (Deuteronomy 26:8). It is that outstretched hand that moved against Jerusalem

---

7. "How Firm a Foundation," *The Presbyterian Hymnal: Hymns, Psalms, and Spiritual Songs* (Louisville: Westminster John Knox, 1990), 361.

"in anger, in fury, and in great wrath" (Jeremiah 21:5). It is that outstretched hand, the act of the creator, who has given all of creation into the hand of Nebuchadnezzar (Jeremiah 27:5-7). And now, in our text, it is that same outstretched hand that will permit restoration and homecoming. What is a taunting reprimand in Isaiah 50:2 becomes, in 59:1, a direct affirmation:

> See, the LORD's hand is not too short to save,
>   nor his ear too dull to hear.

What follows is the insistence that Israel lingers in the zero hour, but not because of divine weakness. It is, in the cadences of the old covenant, because of Israel's "iniquity." The term is used three times in verses 2, 4, 6! Thus the poetic affirmation of verse 1 at the same time "explains" why Israel lingers in disarray and assures that the displacement will end soon because YHWH's uninhibited power is about to be mobilized.

These three divine responses in 40:28-31; 49:15-18; and 50:2-3 serve to override Israel's complaints. We are left with the urgent and exceedingly difficult question of how it is that hope overrides despair. The force of these promissory utterances is to reframe the dismay of Israel and to resituate the imagination of the displaced. As long as the displaced are preoccupied with the palpable causes of despair — the city in shambles, the hegemony of the empire — the utterance of promise is not credible. It is not more than wishful thinking.

It is for that reason that the prophetic tradition takes some care to insist that such primary utterance is not a fantasy or an act of human invention. It is rather, the tradition insists, an utterance that arises "from elsewhere," from the God who indwells the abyss and who initiates a new historical possibility by resolve that is not disrupted by the city in shambles and is not restrained by the force of empire. That claim is stated most succinctly in the formula

"Thus says the LORD." But behind that familiar formula is the poetic imagery of "divine council," a claim that the word arises from beyond.[8] Thus the dialogical interaction of many voices in Isaiah 40:1-11 is taken to be a conversation among the "messengers" who surround the heavenly throne of the creator king. Thus Jeremiah can dismiss his "false" opponents by alleging that they have not had access to "the council," and so have no authorized word (see Jeremiah 23:18, 22). Thus in the poetry of Isaiah, the conventional term for "news" ("message"; *basar*) has morphed into a freighted theological assertion of a word that comes from outside all explanatory categories. The Isaiah tradition employs the term four times:

> Get you up to a high mountain,
>   O Zion, herald of *good tidings*. . .
>   lift it up, do not fear;
> say to the cities of Judah,
>   "Here is your God." (40:9)

> I first have declared it to Zion,
>   and I give to Jerusalem a herald of *good tidings*. (41:27)

> How beautiful on the mountains
>   are the feet of the messenger who announces peace,
> who brings *good news*,
>   who announces salvation,
>   who says to Zion, "Your God reigns." (52:7)

> The spirit of the Lord GOD is upon me,
>   because the LORD has anointed me;
> he has sent me to bring *good news* to the oppressed,

---

8. See Patrick D. Miller, Jr., *Genesis 1-11: Studies in Structure & Theme* (Journal for the Study of the Old Testament Supplement Series 8; Sheffield: JSOT, 1978), 9-26.

> to bind up the brokenhearted,
> to proclaim liberty to the captives,
>   and release to the prisoners;
> to proclaim the year of the LORD's favor,
>   and the day of vengeance of our God. (61:1-2)

The sum of these uses is the insistence that an uttered word matches the verdict taken in the sphere of God *out beyond* human imagination or invention. That utterance (verdict, resolve, "thought" as in 55:8-9) is the way in which the empire-evoked arena of despair is interrupted and contradicted. The Isaiah tradition declares the "news" that eventuates in "comfort" at homecoming. The Jeremiah tradition begins with a mandate to prophetic utterance:

> You shall go to all to whom I send you,
> and you shall speak whatever I command you. (1:7)

And even in Ezekiel, from whom we least anticipate it, it is the word in a God-given scroll that provides the basis for the prophetic work that follows:

> I looked, and a hand was stretched out to me, and a written scroll was in it. He spread it before me; it had writing on the front and on the back, and written on it were words of lamentation and mourning and woe. (Ezekiel 2:9-10)

The great advocate in our time of such divine utterance is Karl Barth, who has understood most clearly that evangelical faith is about speaking and hearing:

> What God said and what God will say is always quite different from what we can and must say to ourselves and others

about its content. . . . the Word of God as directed to us is a Word which we do not say to ourselves and which we could not in any circumstances say to ourselves. . . . The Word of God always tells us something fresh that we had never heard before from anyone.[9]

Barth quotes Luther:

But He keepeth specially before Him two members, ear and tongue; for the kingdom of God is founded upon the Word that one cannot grasp or conceive without these two members, ears and tongue, and ruleth alone through the Word and faith in the hearts of men. The ears grasp the Word and the heart believeth it; but the tongue uttereth or confesseth it as the heart believeth. So if we do away with the tongue and ears, there remaineth no marked difference betwixt the kingdom of Christ and the world.[10]

In sum,

No matter what God's Word says to man *in concretissimo,* it always tells him that he is not his own but God's.[11]

That is the word of the prophetic tradition addressed to Israel in its despair. Israel could imagine that it was its own, without resources. Or it could imagine that it was owned and governed

9. Karl Barth, *Church Dogmatics* I/1 (Edinburgh: T&T Clark, 1975), 141. On the Word of God, see Nicholas Wolterstorff, *Divine Discourse: Philosophical Reflections on the Claim That God Speaks* (Cambridge: Cambridge University Press, 1995).

10. Barth, *Church Dogmatics* I/1, 151.

11. *Church Dogmatics* I/1, 150. Barth's phrasing is an echo of the first answer to the Heidelberg Catechism: "That I belong to my faithful savior Jesus Christ."

by Babylon. But the utterance from God, voiced by the prophets, tells otherwise.

Such a claim for prophetic utterance is of course deeply problematic, because the word in its claim seems weak and unconvincing in a world where despair has such defining power. And of course the empire always wants to silence, nullify, and defeat such utterances. Jacques Ellul has written of the "humiliation of the word," the reduction of public discourse to the "image" that is static, thin, and without transformative power.[12] Thus Isaiah 44:9-20 can detail the ways in which the empire specializes in impotent images. For that reason, it is always a deep contest between transformative utterance and immobilizing image, to which we can say two things: first, that the prophets are undeterred in their assignment. They do not quit! And second, their utterances are effective enough that they regularly evoke and recruit a following, albeit a minority following, that refuses imperial imagery which is the seedbed of despair.

Thus the great eruption of utterance in that abyss of despair became new ground for life for displaced Israel. That historical possibility required "practical" agents like Ezra and Nehemiah. But the trigger for the practical is the defiant, empowering utterance of alternative that is grounded in nothing other than the reality of the God who gives speech. Thus the one who speaks is "the everlasting God" (Isaiah 40:28) who will "never forget" (49:15), whose hand is not shortened (50:2)! All these claims are against the despair that urges, in the zero hour, that God disregards (40:27), that God has forsaken and forgotten (49:15), that God has no power to save (50:2).

Out of this utterance from the one who stands outside the despair system comes a torrent of promises.

12. Jacques Ellul, *The Humiliation of the Word*, trans. Joyce Main Hanks (Grand Rapids: Eerdmans, 1985).

- The tradition of Isaiah is preoccupied with the well-being of Jerusalem, the very city that is now in shambles. This poetry begins with an assurance to the city:

> Speak tenderly to Jerusalem,
>   and cry to her
> that she has served her term,
>   that her penalty is paid,
> that she has received from the LORD's hand
>   double for all her sins. (Isaiah 40:2)

That poetry culminates in 65:17-25 with a vision of the city that is ordered for well-being, thus it is Jeru-*salem*. The poet can imagine that a newness will be enacted like the old Exodus (43:18-19). That emancipatory act, moreover, will issue in an exuberant procession of homecoming that will include those with "weak hands" and "feeble knees" (35:3):

> A highway shall be there,
>   and it shall be called the Holy Way. . .
> No lion shall be here,
>   nor shall any ravenous beast come up on it;
> they shall not be found there,
>   but the redeemed shall walk there.
> And the ransomed of the LORD shall return,
>   and come to Zion with singing;
> everlasting joy shall be on their heads;
>   they shall obtain joy and gladness,
>   and sorrow and sighing shall flee away.
>   (35:8-10; see 55:12-13)

In a very different idiom Jeremiah, schooled in the tradition of Deuteronomy, can imagine a reconstitution of the fractured cov-

enant of Mount Sinai. It is all about Torah obedience, for Torah is
the source of life, the way in which to be deeply in sync with the
creator God who wills forgiveness and reconciliation:

> But this is the covenant that I will make with the house
> of Israel after those days, says the LORD: I will put my law
> within them, and I will write it on their hearts; and I will be
> their God, and they shall be my people . . . for I will forgive
> their iniquity, and remember their sin no more. (Jeremiah
> 31:33-34)

While Jeremiah has Jerusalem on his horizon, it is not his primary focus. He thinks, rather, in terms of the old land that is the
heritage of the covenant community (on which see Jeremiah 32).

In yet a different cadence, Ezekiel can imagine that God's new
future will be a restored, rehabilitated temple. Now the temple
and its altar will be the source of the water of life that will fully
fructify the entire land:

> Then he brought me out by the way of the north gate, and led
> me around on the outside to the outer gate that faces toward
> the east; and the water was coming out on the south side. . . .
> On the banks, on both sides of the river, there will grow all
> kinds of trees for food. Their leaves will not wither nor their
> fruit fail, but they will bear fresh fruit every month, because
> the water for them flows from the sanctuary. Their fruit will
> be for food, and their leaves for healing. (Ezekiel 47:2, 12)

There are great variety and great freedom in this collage of
promissory oracles. We may believe that each prophetic speaker
utilized imagery congruent with his own rootage in a particular
tradition, thus, variously, new city, new covenant, new temple.
In each case, the particularity of the utterance witnesses to a

historical possibility that lies outside what could be imagined in the context of the old city or in the purview of the empire. That utterance, rooted in tradition, grounded in holy resolve, mediated through particular experience, and turned toward the zero hour, is not held back by the force of despair. Despair continues to have its provisional grip, and the force of hope is not guaranteed. But these voices of hope continue in their bold contradiction. They could not do otherwise. And Israel, even in its zero hour, knew itself addressed. It is not easy to embrace the "new math" (new algebra!), but it is possible! The despair can last only so long, only "until . . ." (Jeremiah 27:2, 22)!

III.

Not unlike the society of ancient Jerusalem after the destruction and in the midst of the displacement, our contemporary U.S. society is at the brink of despair. I have said of ancient Jerusalem that it was "near despair," as the buoyant hopefulness of Yahwism guarded against *complete* despair. In our contemporary case, I do not think we have yet reached the point of complete despair — and this because, I suggest, we have managed to sustain our ideology-induced denial. Where denial flourishes, there may not be complete despair!

And yet there are important indications of despair among us, not least the amorphous anxiety that recognizes in inchoate ways that the old world in which we have felt comfortable, safe, and in control is slipping through our fingers. That anxiety is variously directed against Muslims, immigrants, or gays, as though any of these populations were the cause or agent of our world loss.

We may identify two very large grounds for despair that permeate our common life. First, it is clear that our society is based on an extravagant use of fossil fuel that is unsustainable. It is unsustainable because the supply of fossil fuel is noticeably finite, but also because its use, while we still have ample supplies, is massively destructive of the very world we most want to inhabit. The unsustainability of such a political economy of course touches everything; our imperial military enterprise depends upon it, as does our inordinate standard of living that specializes in consumer commodities made possible by cheap labor elsewhere in the world.

Second, it is clear that the modern project of Enlightenment rationality, with its anthropomorphic "turn to the subject," cannot keep its promises of safety and happiness. That "turn to the subject" has benefitted us greatly; it has, however, eventuated in a vigorous individualism that has trivialized the common good, that has reduced major societal needs to technical problems, and that has neglected the infrastructure that is indispensable for a viable common life.

It is clear that limitless, undisciplined use of fossil fuel, coupled with Enlightenment rationality, provides the distorted content of the ideology of American self-perception. It is equally clear that such a package of loyalties and practices have generated a social reality that is remote, for most people, from "the American dream." Our public leadership, almost without exception, has no capacity to imagine outside the categories of these loyalties and commitments. The outcome is the conviction, mostly not articulated, that we are living on borrowed time. As a result, our shrill public discourse is mostly the insistence that we should continue to do what we do, only better, only more vigorously and more adamantly, assuming that if we do so, somehow it will "all work out."

But, of course, our wise despair knows better. And so we have this tension between our professed zeal for continuing what is unsustainable and the hidden broad conviction that in the long run such an effort is futile. We shuttle continually between a broad public pretense and a deep hidden awareness that cannot

Hope amid Despair

be talked about. And while we shuttle, the indices of social health and social well-being among us continue in free fall. That anxious shuttle is the seedbed of despair in which denial is no longer possible, because we know better. While we recite the ideology of chosenness, the underneath realities of our common life expose that ideology as empty of generative power. The more we recite and perform the jingoism of the ideology, the more — in our awareness of unsustainability — we cannot trust the rhetoric.

That despair-generating anxiety is acted out in many ways in our society, of which I will identify five:

- Anxiety is acted out as *unrestrained greed.* The assumption is that we live in a zero-sum game in which there are no more gifts to be given, above all no more fossil fuel. The commitment to self-serving wealth has no limit among us, so that the pyramid of wealth and control flows to the few on the basis of the cheap labor of the many. That greed, moreover, is ruthless and is willing to hurt any neighbor who may impede the success of accumulation.

- Anxiety is acted out as *privatism.* The ideology of greed has now made what is for many a persuasive case that government that pertains to the common good and taxes that finance the public good are an unbearable and unnecessary burden. From that it follows that everything from schools to prisons to health care should be privatized, assuring well-being for those who have sufficient resources, along with a ruthless triage toward those who lack such resources. The advance of the private self — the possessive individual — at the expense of the common good is given visible form in the Tea Party Movement.[13] But in fact, the bent toward privatism is much

13. On the possessive self, see C. B. Macpherson, *The Political Theory of Possessive Individualism: Hobbes to Locke* (Oxford: Clarendon, 1962).

115

broader than that, based on the assumption that the "neighborhood" is an unfortunate inconvenience rather than an indispensable arrangement for viable human life. I suppose that the so-called "survival shows" on television constitute the dramatic performance of privatism in which everything is raw competition, an assumption that lies behind the drama of *The Hunger Games*.

- Anxiety is acted out as *willing violence*. The success of the gun lobby, led by the National Rifle Association, indicates that greed and privatism are prepared to make a ready move to self-protective violence. The shameless readiness of the NRA, in the wake of the tragedy in Newton, Connecticut, to arm everyone is an indication of the profound self-destructive anxiety in our society. That NRA proposal was not met by an appropriately firm rejection by our leaders, but by a caution of cowardice in the face of political risk. The gun lobby is an extreme expression of privatism, in which it is "every man for himself," free to enact violence against anyone who stands in the way. Thus "Stand Your Ground" laws, shot through with macho fear and racism, detract from "the monopoly of force" by the state and allow anyone to practice violence against the neighbor, even with the flimsiest of excuses. Such violence is a feature of privatism that is in the service of greed. Indeed, such violence has become a common assumption of life, expressed variously in eagerness for military combat against any perceived threat, a readiness to torture, and a willingness to execute anyone who offends against the law. There is indeed something ironic and incongruent about the "Right to Life" effort to redefine a fertilized egg as a "person" with protection for the unborn, while all the "born" must make their way in a barbarism of violence.

- Anxiety is acted out as *nostalgia* for "the good old days" of a simpler life. Thus the favorite political portrayal of social life in

the U.S. is still a "mom and pop" venture of small time neighborliness that predictably eschews the complex density of urban life. No doubt Andy Griffith, with his *Mayberry*, might be
the most compelling throwback to face-to-face neighborliness
of a gentle sort. And of course, such nostalgia that wants to
pretend against the reality of urban life that is peopled with
others unlike us is an immense temptation of religious life. The
construction of "Whole Life Centers" by "successful" churches
constitutes a beguiling attempt to live in a safe, protected, ho-
mogeneous community of the like-minded, while fencing out
frightening otherness. And of course, "homeschooling," along
with "private schools," is a handy aid for such a protected, un-
real world. Given the awareness of free fall in our society, one
can sympathize with the plaintive wish, "I just want my world
back." One indication of the sense of loss was the provocative
mantra in the 2012 presidential campaign, "Take back our
country." The slogan reflects the sense that someone has seized
our world from us, not unlike whe way in which the Babylonians seized the world of Jerusalem away from its inhabitants.
Nostalgia is an attempt to recover that world that is gone, if
indeed it ever existed.

· Anxiety performed as greed, privatism, violence, and nostalgia takes place in the presence of a *pervasive sense of "end
time."* Thus a large proportion of current films are now "end
of world" scenarios that recognize and act out the unsustainability of the present arrangement of power, access, and
goods. Such "end-time" anxiety always plays readily into the
hands of religious apocalypticism in which the most aggres-
sively greedy religious enterprises are also the ones that most
loudly proclaim that the end is upon us. Even given that exploitative posture, the preoccupation with "end time" is an
indication that the present world is no longer felt to be sustainable, an awareness that erupted among us on 9/11.

The unsustainability of the present system of power, goods, and access yields a credo that "It is every man for himself" and "You are on your own." These are echoes of Ayn Rand, now become, via Paul Ryan, a major public philosopher among us — for God's sake, a second-rate ideological novelist who sets the tone for public discourse! The disappearance of the common good may seem like a warrant for making it on one's own, except that for very many people right away and for everyone eventually, "You are on your own" is not an affirmation but a threat. The mantra can be reformulated as "We are abandoned." We are left without resources; we are left without a neighborly infrastructure, without the ultimate guarantees of sustaining grace. If I am not mistaken, the outcome of an awareness of an unsustainable rationality of raw individualism is a counterpoint to the old laments I have already cited:

> My way is hidden from the LORD,
>> and my right is disregarded by my God. (Isaiah 40:27)

> The LORD has forsaken me,
>> my LORD has forgotten me. (Isaiah 49:14)

> Is my hand shortened, that it cannot redeem?
>> Or have I no power to deliver? (Isaiah 50:2)

The sinking feeling of free fall is that

- My way is disregarded;
- I am forgotten and forsaken;
- The saving hand is short.

We do not, of course, voice this matter in such direct theological cadences. But the intent and effect are the same. The loss of old Jerusalem left the survivors bereft, with "All that I had hoped for from the LORD" gone (Lamentations 3:18). In our time, it is free fall; it is free fall without resources, thus witness the current drama of triage among us in every dimension of our public life, including health care, education, libraries, and even grocery stores. And even among those with resources, the chance for private shalom is nil when the public good evaporates. Whether this abandonment is voiced in direct theological cadences as in ancient Israel or whether it is among us left inchoate, the outcome is the same: an unbearable loss of world. Or as Ezra belatedly stated in his prayer:

> Here we are, slaves to this day — slaves in the land that you gave to our ancestors to enjoy its fruit and its good gifts. Its rich yield goes to the kings whom you have set over us because of our sins; they have power also over our bodies and over our livestock at their pleasure, and we are in great distress. (Nehemiah 9:36-37)

His prayer is addressed to God. But Ezra's words constitute an acute economic analysis. Ezra's prayer is an act of hope — but barely! He comes near to despair but not quite, because he continues to pray. He voices the powerlessness of his community. His final word is "distress" — as is ours in this unsustainable circumstance.

IV.

In the midst of near-despair, the prophetic task is to articulate hope, the prospect of fresh historical possibility assured by God's good governance of the future. The prophetic utterance of promise to the displaced in sixth-century Israel was completely inexplicable, except by the recognition that the word of promise came "from elsewhere," from the verdict and resolve of YHWH. In parallel fashion, utterance of promise in the midst of world loss in our time is completely inexplicable, except it be given "from elsewhere." It is not necessary to have a particular notion of "inspiration and revelation" to make such a claim; all that is required is the awareness that such an utterance might engage the speaker as much as the listener. Such utterance arises in a way that contradicts the evident facts on the ground, contradicts what the listener expected to hear, and contradicts what the speaker intended to say. Thus as despair knows about world loss in our time, so the work of hope is to conjure and imagine an alternative world now to be given "from elsewhere."

Since I have proceeded in my argument by an analogy from ancient Israel to contemporary U.S. society, I dare one more analogy that may illuminate the work of hope. Jonathan Lear has written a remarkable reflection on the life and destiny of Plenty Coups, the last great chief of the Crow nation of Native Americans, poignantly entitled *Radical Hope*.[14]

The first part of Lear's book focuses on the loss and diminishment of the Crow Nation as it succumbed to white settlers and the enforcement of the white government when "the buffalo went away." Plenty Coups told Lear that after that "nothing happened." History ended, memory ceased, "the hearts of my people fell to the ground and they could not lift them up again. There was little singing anywhere."[15] The mood of these statements is not unlike those of ancient Israel: "By the rivers of Babylon — there we sat down and there we wept" (Psalm 137:1). The Crow experienced this as death of established social roles, of standards of excel-

14. Jonathan Lear, *Radical Hope: Ethics in the Face of Cultural Devastation* (Cambridge, MA: Harvard University Press, 2006).
15. Lear, *Radical Hope*, 3.

lence, and of personal identities.[16] It is for good reason that the nation lost its sense of life, meaning, and energy. In his section tellingly entitled "Reasoning at the Abyss," Lear reports that the Crow entered a time when everything familiar and reliable ceased and they were required "to live a life that I do not understand."[17]

But what interests us in Lear's account is not the descent into the abyss, a descent like that of sixth-century Israel. Our topic here is hope, that is, the prospect of a future for the Crow Nation. That prospect takes the form of a dream that Plenty Coups had that was received, processed, and interpreted by the tribal elders.

The substance of the dream, hypothesized by Lear, affirmed that:

- all our traditional way of life is coming to an end . . . that life is about to disappear;
- we must do what we can to open our imaginations up to a radically different set of future possibilities;
- I need to recognize the discontinuity that is upon me . . . I need to preserve some integrity across that discontinuity;
- I do have reason to hope for a dignified passage across this abyss, because God — Ah-badt-dadt-deah — is good;
- we shall get the good back, though at the moment we have no more than a glimmer of what that might mean.[18]

Lear concludes about the reasoning of Plenty Coups:

It is committed to the bare idea *that something good will emerge.* But it does so in recognition that one's thick understandings of the good life are about to disappear. It thereby

16. Lear, *Radical Hope*, 42.
17. Lear, *Radical Hope*, 56, 61.
18. Lear, *Radical Hope*, 92-94.

manifests a commitment to the idea that the goodness of the world transcends one's limited and vulnerable attempt to understand it. There is no implication that one can glimpse what lies beyond the horizons of one's historically situated understanding. There is no claim to grasp ineffable truths. Indeed, this form of commitment is impressive in part because it acknowledges that no such grasp is possible. Even so, this form of reasoning shows that a very peculiar form of commitment is possible and intelligible: namely, that although Plenty Coups can recognize that his understanding of self and world is based on a set of living commitments that are vulnerable, it is nevertheless possible to commit to a goodness that transcends that understanding.[19]

That substance is matched by an awareness that the medium of this hope is a dream that is elusive and without clarity, thus requiring interpretation. That sense of the dream is a huge "if":

If the dream comes from a divine source *and* it tells us that our way of life will come to an end *and* it tells us how to survive the destruction of our traditional way of life, we should expect that there is much about the message and much about the future that we do not yet understand. Still, the message purports to come from an absolute source; and that kind of authority could conceivably provide something to hold onto in the face of overwhelming challenge.[20]

The sure sense is that the dream comes "from elsewhere." As in the Bible and in many folk societies, dreams are understood as disclosures given with absolute divine authority, the kind of ab-

19. Lear, *Radical Hope*, 94-95.
20. Lear, *Radical Hope*, 91.

soluteness that makes the encoded message reliable, even if not immediately transparent.

Lear comments on this hope rooted in the dream:

> For Plenty Coups the question of hope was intimately bound to the question of how to live. . . . Thus the issue of hope becomes crucial for an ethical inquiry into life at the horizons of one's understanding.[21]

The dream gave assurance:

> Plenty Coups made a claim: that if the tribe adhered to the dream they would face an inevitable devastation but they would survive. Indeed, they would come out the other side with new ways to live well. . . . Thus his capacity to have that dream and to stick to its meaning is a manifestation of courage.[22]

The dream turned out to be a guide and an experiment to seek a new way of living in the world, a new way that avoided both the resignation of despair and the suicide of resistance to white power, the latter an option taken by other tribes. Thus the dream permits a third way between resignation and destruction:

> Thus I think the case is made not just that it was psychologically advantageous not to give in to despair but also that it would have been a mistake to do so. It would also have been a mistake to "go down fighting." The aim was not merely the biological survival of the individual members of the tribe — however important that was — but the future flourishing of

21. Lear, *Radical Hope*, 105.
22. Lear, *Radical Hope*, 113.

traditional tribal values, customs, and memories in a new context.[23]

Thus the abyss between the old ways that ended and the new ways yet to emerge is now occupied by the dream, an elusive, God-given assurance that required trust in its reliability.

This way of positioning the dream between the old that had failed and the new that is awaited is pivotal for Lear's rendering of the work of Plenty Coups. This act of hope by the Crow Nation on the basis of the dream is indeed

> the assurance of things hoped for, the conviction of things not seen. (Hebrews 11:1)

It takes no great transfiguration to see that the same structure of hope in abyss is how the faith of Israel was shaped in the utterance of Israel's sixth-century poets. The grief of Lamentations had brought them candidly to the abyss. And the work of reconstruction would begin soon enough. But the crisis in near-despair is that long moment of free fall between. It is that moment that the poet parses in the double use of "moment":

> . . . for a brief moment . . .
> for a moment. (Isaiah 54:7-8)

That moment could not be filled with plans or blueprints or schedules or budgets or creeds or "six easy steps." It can only be filled by that which God gives. And what God gives is elusive at best. Among the Crow Nation, it was a dream. The dream filled the void and provided substance amid free fall. In the sixth century it is

---

23. Lear, *Radical Hope*, 145.

song, narrative, and oracle, utterance that is elusive but that is taken to be God-given.

Later on Jerusalem would be reshaped around the Torah so that political power was displaced by Torah piety. But that is later on. Before such specificity, God-given elusiveness is the order of the day. Thus I formulate what Lear traces and what Israel's poets offer in this way:

- Hope is a tenacious act of imagination given in dream, oracle, narrative, and song, rooted in absolute authority concerning divine purpose.
- It is an act of playful imagination with ill-defined and open images that suggest without clarity.
- It is given in an imaginative way, because it is out beyond what we know.
- It is enacted with tenacity; the poets defied "reality" and settled authority in order to voice reality out beyond present arrangements.
- It is, in an audacious claim, said to be the very word of God, the word that "will stand forever" (Isaiah 40:8), the word that will "accomplish that which I purpose" (Isaiah 55:11), a word that is "in your mouth a fire" (Jeremiah 5:14), that cannot be held in (Jeremiah 20:9).

That word, enacted in ancient Israel and mediated to Plenty Coups, contradicts all known reality. It summons out beyond the known that is lost. It assures in the midst of free fall that "the end" will not prevail. It anticipates newness not yet in hand.

From this analysis I suggest that the prophetic task now, in contemporary U.S. society, is exactly to perform hope that is characteristically a tenacious act of imagination, grounded in a dream, song, narrative, or oracle, rooted in the elusive but faithful authority of God. The prophet is the one who dares to speak such a future that is out beyond all evidence. The work is not simply to reiterate old acts of hope, but to be informed by such old acts in order to perform acts that may be grounded in divine initiative.

It is an obvious move to go from the dream of Plenty Coups to the dream of Martin Luther King, Jr. What happened when the old poets said "Thus says the Lord" and when Plenty Coups told his dream to the elders is precisely what happened when King reported his dream:

> I have a dream that one day this nation will rise up and live out the true meaning of its creed: "We hold these truths to be self-evident, that all men are created equal."
>
> I have a dream that one day on the red hills of Georgia the sons of former slaves and the sons of former slave owners will be able to sit down together at the table of brotherhood.
>
> I have a dream that one day even the state of Mississippi, a desert state sweltering with the heat of injustice, sweltering with the heat of oppression, will be transformed into an oasis of freedom and justice.
>
> I have a dream that my four little children will one day live in a nation where they will not be judged by the color of their skin but by the content of their character.
>
> I have a dream today.[24]

As narrated, the dream is an act of tenacious imagination by King, who risked everything and would not quit. It is a poetic scenario without specificity; and surely King himself had no notion of how to implement the dream. It is, without ever saying so, rooted

24. Martin Luther King, Jr., "I Have a Dream," in *Sociology of Religion: A Reader*, ed. Susanne C. Monahan, William Mirola, and Michael O. Emerson (Upper Saddle River, NJ: Prentice Hall, 2001), 404-6.

in the absoluteness of God's purpose. The dream is that of King. But before King, it is God's own dream of new reality. What King does is fill the space in the liminal season of U.S. life between old failed racism and new human community with the cadences of possibility.

The utterance is filled with the implied authority of God that gives the vision moral authority of an intense kind. Indeed, the legislation that followed King's address which has shaped public life gives the lie to W. H. Auden's dictum that poetry does nothing. This poetry — dream, song, narrative, oracle — does a great deal. It provides staying power, moral energy, and courage for the deep season of abyss. It breeds fresh historical possibility in the zero hour.

In the horizon of Plenty Coups, the dreamed possibility was a life other than the old nomadic one that could not be sustained. In ancient Israel, for the poets,

- It was with Jeremiah a new covenantal community.
- It was with Isaiah a new city of shalom.
- It was with Ezekiel a new cleansed temple filled with presence.

And now the prophetic task is not blueprint or program or even advocacy. It is the elusiveness of possibility out beyond evidence, an act of imagination that authorizes the listening assembly to imagine even out beyond the ken of the speaker.

In this liminal moment of abyss in our society, prophetic imagination

- may now dream of possibilities for peace and justice with lesser measures of U.S. hegemony;
- may now dream of a lowered standard of living among us, but with a genuine neighborliness in which all share;
- may now dream of a new cultural pluralism in which the

marker is not nation, race, ethnic origin, but the capacity for neighborliness;

- may now dream of a religious ecumenism in which particular faith is deeply held in the presence of other deeply held faiths.

What emerges on the lips of the poet is a new world now being given and now being received.

This way of hope is the work of ministry. Doing advocacy for good causes is urgent. But more urgent, in my view, is the nurture of venues of obedient imagination in which unuttered possibility is uttered, thoughts beyond our thoughts are thought, and ways beyond our ways are known (Isaiah 55:8-9). In such circumstance, walking by sight is likely a return to the old ways that have failed. Walking by faith is to seek a world other than the one from which we are being swiftly ejected (Hebrews 11:14).

V

Living amid Empire as Neighborhood

The prophetic task, in our time as in ancient time, summons the community of faith to make knowing and risky decisions between options of life or death. I have lined out the two narratives that stand before us as they did that ancient people. In what follows I propose to sketch out, as starkly as I can, the issues to which the church is now summoned in our society. Decisions of a quite practical kind that run against the grain of the dominant narrative are always risky. So it is with us. The church and its ministry, along with our culture more generally, are situated between two competing narratives that contradict each other. Each of them is offered as a metanarrative that provides an adequate explanatory account of our life and presents itself as so elemental as to preclude other claims of explanation. The fact that we are caught between the two and do not want to choose between them constitutes a profound crisis for us generally, a crisis that is visible in the church as in larger society. Because of that crisis we may usefully expend critical energy in identifying and characterizing these two narratives and participate in the on-going unresolved (and irresolvable?) sorting out of these competing claims.

These two narratives, which may be variously characterized, I identify as:

1. *the totalizing narrative of the empire,* and
2. *the particularizing narrative of the neighborhood.*

The two narratives are intermingled and confused among us in ways that produce tension and conflict.

My thought is that such intermingling and confusion result in stress and fatigue as we practice juggling and denial in order not to come to terms with the contradiction. In the end, I judge, that intermingling and confusion eventuate in the deep disability that continues to vex both church and society. The pastoral task, it may follow, is to sort out these narratives and their claims, as pertains to

- the body politic and public policy,
- the body of the church, and
- our personal lives amid the contradiction.

I can think of three ways in which the two narratives are commonly intermingled:

1. In the mantra of "God and country," we enact a confusion of "the American way of life" with the gospel. Indeed, it seems clear that sorting out this long-standing, uncriticized ideological assumption is part of our most urgent and most difficult task. And of course the pervasive militarization of our society continues to generate more energy to sustain the confusion, so that it is difficult even to raise the question. This confusion inevitably transposes the ideology of nationalism (and its present expression as a National Security State) into a gospel claim.

2. We face the intermingling of secular ideology (which serves market ideology, the pyramid of economic accumulation with its aggressive initiatives) with an evangelical façade. As a result, secular claims are voiced in ways that sound like evangelical faith. This uncriticized alliance on the one hand makes for great "church growth," as worship of the idea of a "strong and free America" is a big dream. At the same time on the other hand, the alliance serves and supports the most aggressive imperial mili-

tarism of our government with the intent of unmitigated access to global markets and resources. All of that is carried out in the name of Jesus, who is now popularly transmitted through the odd formulations of Ayn Rand.

3. A more benign but equally problematic formulation of the intermingling is found in the popular mantra, "I am spiritual but not religious." That mantra functions to declare freedom from any defining theological tradition, the absence of any inconvenient missional mandate that finally ends in religious narcissism. One does not need to be an apologist for the institutional church with its long history of wounding in order to see that such a "disembodied" notion of religion is simply a new form of Gnosticism that leaves the status quo of society untroubled and unquestioned.

All of the formulations — "God and country," secularism with an evangelical façade, and "spiritual but not religious" — attest to the urgency of the task of thinking again about these competing contradictory claims to an ultimate narrative. In what follows, I will exposit, as best I can, the two narratives and then reflect on the urgent practice of adjudication and advocacy amid such confusion.

I.

The first candidate for metanarrative that we consider is "the totalizing narrative of the empire." I have learned from James Boyd White, via Simone Weil with reference to the *Iliad*, that "empire" is always about "force." White writes about "the empire of force," an empire of aggressive predation.[1] That force, characteristically, consists in these elements:

1. James Boyd White, *Living Speech: Resisting the Empire of Force* (Princeton: Princeton University Press, 2006).

1. The economy, organized as a pyramid, so that money flows to the center of the empire, to the apex of the pyramid, to the managers who make the money rules — most usually a collusion of church, state, and corporation. Thus in our most recent economic drama, resources were mobilized precisely to "save the banks."

2, Political monologue that eliminates all voices from below, that settles for a narrow consensus of opinion to the exclusion of other opinion. This is an exclusion that drifts toward fascism and that erodes, if not eliminates, democratic possibility. In our society that monologue is abetted by "mainstream" media that collude with and support the consensus of the governing class.

3. One-dimensional religion that is absent of any critical edge. The dominant economic, political system requires the reduction of "god" to a settled object of allegiance that lacks any freedom of agency, a reduction that is both permitted and required by Enlightenment rationality that could not, on "rational" grounds, imagine divine agency and that could not, on political grounds, tolerate such agency.

The practical outcome of the combination of an economy of pyramid, a politics of monologue, and a religion of objectivity is the reduction of the identity of participants in such a systemic arrangement to "consumers" who contribute to the economic process of pyramid, who assent to the political process, and who willingly agree to theological reduction on the assumption that maintenance will assure a livable life. The immediate cost of reduction of identity to consumer is the disappearance of the participatory citizen and, consequently, the loss of any public dimension to social reality and the forfeiture of the common good. This reduction, required and legitimated by the imperial narrative, was given classic expression by Margaret Thatcher: "There is no such thing as society; there is only the market." More recent articulation is by Ron Paul, who, in the name of "liberty," wants to create an open field for predation without any acknowledgement of those who are so disadvantaged and so "left behind" that they cannot possibly benefit from such much-taunted liberty. The outcome is cheap labor that has neither the will nor the means to embrace agency on its own behalf.

In the Bible, Pharaoh, in the book of Exodus, is the icon for the narrative of empire. The pyramids of Pharaoh are a reliable and authentic totem of empire in which cheap labor (slaves) is engaged in the endless rat race of productivity with profits flowing to the top, to the benefit of Pharaoh and his company. On the one hand, the slaves are engaged in building "supply cities" (Exodus 1:11), that is, depositories for Pharaoh's surplus that amounts to a monopoly (see Genesis 47:13-26). Our contemporary equivalent would be the "great banks" which, in their greedy predation, have made economic viability improbable for vulnerable cheap labor. On the other hand, Pharaoh's endless demand for an escalated production schedule is insatiable (Exodus 5:6-19). As is characteristic in such a social arrangement, the pyramid managers decry the inadequate performance of cheap labor with accusations of moral failure:

> He said, "You are lazy, lazy; that is why you say, 'Let us go and sacrifice to the LORD.' Go now, and work; for no straw shall be given to you, but you shall still deliver the same number of bricks." (Exodus 5:17-18)

This articulation is an early indictment that is currently echoed in the analysis of Charles Murray, in which the "have nots" do not measure up socially and morally to the high standards of the managers of the pyramid.[2]

I have elsewhere termed Pharaoh's system (which is repli-

---

2. Charles Murray, *Coming Apart: The State of White America, 1960-2010* (New York: Crown Forum, 2012).

cated in our contemporary National Security State) as a system of "therapeutic, technological, consumerist militarism," the goal of which is the sustenance and enhancement of an unsustainable standard of living for the few at the expense of the vulnerable many.[3] In such a narrative, the accumulation of food ("consumerism"!), money, power, and control is the aim of enterprise. Such accumulation, it is assumed, will make us happy and safe.[4] Such accumulation, moreover, requires a strong military, because the process consists in living off the cheap labor of others and taking from them what properly belongs to them.

The narrative of empire may be exposited in the following ways, though the dimensions of the narrative that I identify are not complete or comprehensive:

1. The narrative of empire is now a major preoccupation of New Testament scholarship, as the self-legitimating narrative of the Roman Empire collides with the ministry of Jesus and with the advocacy of Paul:

- Richard Horsley, in a series of studies, has identified the ways in which Jesus critiques the power of Rome in the interest of safe living space for his own Jewish community. He traces the forceful, violent policies of Rome to impose its rule on a subject people. And he concludes of Jesus:

  It is surely in the role of a prophet leading a popular movement that Jesus, like his paradigmatic predecessors Moses and Elijah, performed healings and exorcisms that manifested the victory of God's rule over that of the Romans. In all of these respects, Jesus of Nazareth belongs in the same

3. Walter Brueggemann, "Living with the Elusive God," *Christian Century* 122/24 (November 29, 2005): 22-28.

4. On "safe and happy," see John Brueggemann, *Rich, Free, and Miserable: The Failure of Success in America* (Lanham: Rowman & Littlefield, 2010).

context with and stands shoulder to shoulder with the other leaders of movements among the Judean and Galilean people, and pursues the same general agenda in parallel paths: independence from Roman imperial rule so that the people can again be empowered to renew their traditional way of life under the rule of God.[5]

· Neil Elliott, in a remarkable argument, has proposed that Paul's intent in the Epistle to the Romans, is, point by point, to counter the claims of Rome and its imperial narrative. In an appeal to the categories of James C. Scott, Elliott traces in turn the force of a) the hidden transcript of the dominant power with reference to Nero, b) the public transcript of Nero's power, and c) the hidden transcript of Paul in Romans that asserts the rule of Jesus as the only legitimate rule, thus delegitimizing Rome.[6] Elliott, moreover, carries the argument of Paul's contradiction of the imperial power to the context of Christian congregations amid the U.S. Empire:

> From an ideological-critical viewpoint, however, other questions must precede — and relativize — the rush to determine "what we can preach":

· In what ways have U.S. churches been shaped by the ideological pressures of a globalizing capitalist culture?
· To what extent have churches incorporated the values of the "civilization of wealth"?
· How do the churches function within a larger ideological system to channel the potentially volatile energy of religious symbols away from conflict with the mechanisms of power?

---

5. Richard A. Horsley, *Jesus and Empire: The Kingdom of God and the New World Disorder* (Minneapolis: Fortress, 2003), 104.

6. Neil Elliott, *The Arrogance of Nations: Reading Romans in the Shadow of Empire* (Minneapolis: Fortress, 2008), 28-57.

- How do the privatization of the churches, their co-optation into the routines of the civil religion, and their careful maintenance of the boundaries assigned to them by the dominant capitalist order (for example, the scrupulous avoiding of speaking against one or another war from the pulpit) effectively domesticate those symbols?
- How do these considerations determine the scope of any preaching to effect needed change in perceptions, attitudes, and practices?[7]

Elliott is uncompromising about the ideological struggle in which Paul is engaged, and in which the contemporary church follows suit.

- Brigitte Kahl has reread Paul's Epistle to the Galatians in a way that understands "Galatians" as a term referring to those who dissent from and refuse Roman law and Roman ordering. She concludes that the epistle is a manifesto summoning to such dissent:

   What Paul rediscovers and radically restates are the exodus foundations of biblical monotheism in the global age of Caesar — and in the new age of the worldwide Jewish Messiah. The "idols" as the intolerable other of Israel's God according to the first and second commandments (Exod. 20:1-6) for Paul may have no longer appeared as simply the equivalent of "other religions" and "paganism" as such. At a time when Roman imperial religion congeals the polytheism of the vanquished nations in a quasi-monotheistic top, Paul "sees" how behind the manifold false and forbidden images of other gods, and even in the imageless worship of Israel's one God, the "Egyptian" *eidolon* of imperial idolatry and ideology pops

7. Elliott, *The Arrogance of Nations*, 165.

up everywhere, *divus* Caesar and *diva* Rome. Like the biblical arch-idol of the golden calf, which was manufactured by the exodus people themselves right at Mount Sinai, the idolatrous image is hailed as God of freedom while it represents the "false gods" of slavery. Monotheism and syncretism get a new meaning. A novel type of hybrid "monotheistic syncretism from below" based justice and survival ruptures the imperial web of power and its "imperial-syncretistic monotheism from above."[8]

Along with dissent, Kahl puts accent on the positive alternative that Paul articulates with reference to the gospel of Jesus:

Yet Paul does not exclusively and not even primarily target the negative of the imperial idol and its order; rather, at the center of his argument is the new messianic community. His insistence on the oneness of God is the claim of human self and human other becoming one in Christ again, through the "birth canal" of divine self-othering at the cross. . . . Only in this messianic community that embodies the *other* law can God be truly worshiped and served as the singular one God who is other than Caesar and thus reconciles self and other in a noncompetitive and nonhierarchical body of "new life."[9]

The sum of this New Testament scholarship, to which other studies could readily be added, is that the Jesus movement embodied a vigorous, emancipated alternative to Rome. In these scholarly projects, the parallel to our own time and place is some-

8. Brigitte Kahl, *Galatians Re-Imagined: Reading with the Eyes of the Vanquished* (Minneapolis: Fortress, 2010), 287-88.

9. Kahl, *Galatians Re-Imagined*, 288-89.

times explicit, more often implicit. But the point is everywhere the same. The imperial narrative of the National Security State, ancient or contemporary, is no adequate script for authentic humanness. The gospel narrative of the messianic community, with its solidarity with the poor, bespeaks an alternative economics, an alternative politics, and an alternative religion.

2. Our contemporary embodiment of the same imperialism has been well articulated by Chalmers Johnson. In his several studies he has exposed the militarization of the entire social system of the United States, so that military investments skew the economy and military ideology preempts religious claims. In his critique of empire, Johnson suggests that among "the sorrows of empire" are the recurring social realities that come with empire.[10] Among them he identifies

- endless taxation all the way to bankruptcy in order to fund the project;
- perpetual war because the empire is always under threat;
- loss of civil rights in order to protect the "secrets" of the empire; and
- assault against homosexuals.

Johnson observes that these practices are recurring, every time reflecting the deeply felt insecurity of empire, even while the empire has near monopoly of power. The totalizing narrative of empire draws its subjects (that is, us!) into acceptance of these practices as "normal and unexceptional." And when the claims become totalizing, they become immune to criticism.

3. I have taken the term "totalizing" from Robert Lifton, the Harvard psychiatrist who has spent his scholarly life studying

---

10. Chalmers Johnson, *The Sorrows of Empire: Militarism, Secrecy, and the End of the Republic* (New York: Metropolitan, 2004).

the causes and effects of atrocity-producing social systems.[11] His study of the German-Polish death camps, Hiroshima, the outcomes of the Vietnam war, and the psychic costs of the nuclear threat are now all summarized in his autobiography, *Witness to an Extreme Century.* Lifton describes the systems that produce the atrocities as "totalizing," by which he means a coercive unwillingness to tolerate any dissent or any pursuit of meaning that falls outside the control of the regime.

Lifton identifies "eight deadly sins" that recur in such totalizing systems:

- milieu control;
- mystical manipulation;
- the demand for purity;
- the cult of confession;
- the sacred science;
- loading the language;
- doctrine over person;
- the dispensing of existence for dispensable people.[12]

The reader may judge the extent to which these "sins" operate in our current imperial narrative. It strikes me, at the least, that among the pertinent elements of this list for our society are the demand for "purity" (concerning gays and lesbians), the cult of confession with an endless parade of transgressive political figures, the loading of language by the use of euphemisms and appeal to religious authority, and the dispensing with poor people as dispensable. I do not suggest that such lethal imperial practice is as "advanced" in our society as in

11. Robert Jay Lifton, *Witness to an Extreme Century: A Memoir* (New York: Free Press, 2011).
12. Lifton, *Witness to an Extreme Century,* 67-68, 381.

others that Lifton has studied. It is, however, advanced enough that we can identify the lethal potential of the imperial narrative among us.

4. Finally, I want to consider the outcomes of the imperial narrative when it is taken as the ordering account of social reality. I make a leap back to Paul's inventories of the "works of the flesh," which, in this context, may be understood not as "natural" modes of conduct, but rather modes that are the assumed and legitimated patterns of behavior in the midst of the imperial narrative. Thus Kahl can say of Paul's list of the "works of the flesh" in Galatians:

> The "works of the flesh" (*erga tēs sarkos*, 5:19) are spelled out in a list of vices (5:19-21) that show an exceptionally strong emphasis on community conflicts and tensions. As the conflict-provoking "works of the flesh" according to 5:21 constitute a practice *(prassontes)* that excludes people from the kingdom (or empire) of God, they are tantamount to the "works of the law" as a social practice that in our reading is equivalent to the combat order of Caesar's empire.[13]

These works reflect the "combat order" of the empire that is inimical to the gospel:

> Now the works of the flesh are obvious: fornication, impurity, licentiousness, idolatry, sorcery, enmities, strife, jealousy, anger, quarrels, dissension, factions, envy, drunkenness, carousing, and things like these. (Galatians 5:19-21)

Other inventories in derivative Pauline literature include the following:

13. Kahl, *Galatians Re-Imagined*, 270.

Put away from you all bitterness and wrath and anger and wrangling and slander, together with all malice. . . . But fornication and impurity of any kind, or greed, must not even be mentioned among you . . . Entirely out of place is obscene, silly, and vulgar talk . . . no fornicator or impure person, or one who is greedy (that is, an idolater) has any inheritance in the kingdom of Christ and of God. (Ephesians 4:31; 5:3-5)

Put to death, therefore, whatever in you is earthly: fornication, impurity, passion, evil desire, and greed (which is idolatry). (Colossians 3:5)

Kahl speaks of competitiveness. It requires no imagination to see the outcomes of such totalizing assumptions in our society with acute negativity toward "the other" and a need to prevail, examples of which include road rage, mean-spiritedness in sitcoms and TV programs designed for children, violence in sports with an accent on virility, especially in beer commercials, and a generic readiness to dismiss the other as an insignificant element in one's own life.

The sum of this pervasive evidence suggests a culture that has come to accept the claims of empire and a readiness to regard those claims as a given which has its own moral staying power that puts those claims beyond criticism. When we consider an evangelical alternative to these totalizing claims, a beginning point is the recognition that the imperial narrative is not an ontological given. It is, rather, from the ground up a carefully constructed, frequently reiterated narrative that is in the service of the pyramid managers. When it is seen as a construct, it follows that our social experience is then open to an alternative construction. But this narrative is the one we inhale on a regular basis, a narrative that is committed to greed, accumulation, and violence that pertains equally to liberals and conservatives. That narrative, moreover, is wrapped in the loud claims of exceptionalism that becomes the air we breathe, surely at great cost to our personal health and to our public possibilities.

II.

The second candidate for metanarrative that I identify is "the particularizing narrative of the neighborhood." On the specificity of "neighborhood" for this narrative, I commend the manifesto of Peter Block and John McKnight, *The Abundant Community*.[14] But of course the Mosaic Torah, well ahead of contemporary scholarship, contended that the neighborhood is the most elemental unit of social meaning. The Bible characteristically bears witness to the formation and maintenance of human living space that is free from the pathologies of empire. Thus:

1. The Exodus narrative is a repeatable liturgical performance that seeks living space outside the totalizing regime of Pharaoh:

   Go to Pharaoh; for I have hardened his heart and the heart of his officials, in order that I may show these signs of mine among them, and that you may tell your children and grandchildren how I have made fools of the Egyptians and what signs I have done among them — so that you may know that I am the LORD. (Exodus 10:1-2)

2. The prophets characteristically seek living space outside the claims and control of the royal-priestly urban hegemony of Jerusalem.

14. John L. McKnight and Peter Block, *The Abundant Community: Awakening the Power of Families and Neighborhoods* (San Francisco: Berrett-Koehler, 2010).

3. Jesus characteristically seeks living space outside the demand
society of Rome.

In each of these cases, the biblical text itself is an act of contestation against the totalizing claim of the regime that is called into
question.

This alternative narrative is characteristically told and enacted
"from below." It arises from the bodily reality of suffering and
exploitation. It is manifested in nonconformist conduct, and it
is geared to specific human reality on the ground among those
who have found the large universalizing claims of the imperial
narrative to be false, toxic, and finally lethal.

While voiced "from below," however, at the same time it is clear
that the distinctive mark of this narrative from below is that it is
occupied and defined by the character of this God, YHWH. YHWH
is apart from and distinct from imperial gods, refuses to participate in the smooth memos and comprehensive syllabi of empire,
but regularly disrupts that narrative in the performance of poem,
song, oracle, and narrative. There is no single summary of the
defining cruciality of YHWH for this counternarrative, but one
case in point is the oracular declaration of Moses:

> For the LORD your God is God of gods and Lord of lords,
> the great God, mighty and awesome, who is not partial and
> takes no bribe, who executes justice for the orphan and the
> widow, and who loves the strangers, providing them food
> and clothing. (Deuteronomy 10:17-18)

Against the claims of Egyptian and/or Canaanite gods, Moses
attests that YHWH is indeed sovereign, as God of gods, Lord of
lords who presides over the divine council. But then there is a
departure from any ordinary doxology. YHWH is characterized
as engaging the fray of human particularity concerning social

justice, attentiveness to the vulnerable, and preoccupied with the quotidian necessities of food and clothing, especially to the vulnerable who are without other resources.

The contrast with the narrative of empire is complete:

1. Unlike the centralized economy of the empire where all flows to the top, the economy of this narrative features miracles of abundance that are unexpectedly and inscrutably given among the lowly. A key agent of such an economy of abundance, for example, is Elisha, an uncredentialed nobody who provided life-sustaining gifts for a resourceless widow who was about to be devoured by predatory economic arrangement.

> So she left him and shut the door behind her and her children; they kept bringing vessels to her, and she kept pouring. When the vessels were full, she said to her son, "Bring me another vessel." But he said to her, "There are no more." (2 Kings 4:5-6)

The narrative does not generalize. It does not assert any general principle. It only tells what happened at this one time to this one mother. We are left in awe. And then belatedly, it is clear that the narratives of Elisha are in great measure reperformed by Jesus, yet again with the same specificity and without any universalizing insistence.

2. Unlike the monologic politics of empire, the politics of this narrative is dialogic. Thus at the very outset of the Exodus narrative, the exploited slaves become subjects of their own history by sounding their insistent voice in a way that evokes the disruptive intervention of YHWH on their behalf into the totalizing system of Pharaoh. As a result, Israel can remember the names of the two midwives who helped birth their children of the future but has no interest in recalling the name of Pharaoh (Exodus 1:15). The process of the narrative (and of subsequent remembering in Israel)

is that those who are reduced to slave or consumer may become recovered, emancipated selves. One can see that same practice in the life of a congregation wherein people are known and named, who have their birthdays and anniversaries remembered, who have their sicknesses and deaths honored, all gestures that call out an affirmed, empowered personhood.[15]

3. Unlike the "objective" religion of the empire, this narrative features an engaged, interactive, subjective faith. The God of this narrative is impacted by the prayers of the faithful. Thus lament, complaint, and protest are legitimate ways to interrupt the thin doxologies of the empire by giving voice to the burdened particularity of daily life. The God of this narrative is drawn into that burdened dailyness in transformative ways.

It is clear, moreover, that this practice of an alternative, seen clearly in Old Testament texts, is reenacted in the narrative of Jesus:

1. The economy of abundance is featured in the "feeding miracles" wherein five loaves and two fish are enough for five thousand men, plus women and children. (Matthew 14:21).

2. The politics of dialogue is evident in the awareness of Jesus that he has been "touched" in a way that emits transformative power (Mark 5:30). That same demanding interaction is performed in the narrative wherein the outsider woman can challenge Jesus so that she becomes a member of the household; indeed, she becomes Jesus' teacher concerning his vocation (Mark 7:28).[16]

3. The subjective practice of religion is commended in Jesus' parable of "the importunate widow" who is a voice "from below" who incessantly addresses power (Luke 18:1-8).

15. See Thomas L. Brodie, *The Crucial Bridge: The Elijah-Elisha Narrative as an Interpretive Synthesis of Genesis-Kings and a Literary Model for the Gospels* (Collegeville: Liturgical, 2000).

16. See Elisabeth Schüssler Fiorenza, *But She Said: Feminist Practices of Biblical Interpretation* (Boston: Beacon, 1992).

In each case, Jesus, like his Old Testament antecedents, shatters conventional propriety and legitimates alternative practice that arises from below. In this practice, he both exposes the inadequacy of empire and gives an invitation to the neighborhood. In the parlance of the church, the new selves of emancipated urgency are baptized persons. In the rhetoric of ancient Israel, they are members of the covenantal community that maintains a distinct identity and a distinct practice in the face of empire.

This counternarrative that disrupts imperial narrative focuses upon particular persons in daily crises, naming, valuing, and empowering persons who have been disregarded, reduced, or summarized by the empire:

- In the Exodus narrative, it is the naming and valuing of the midwives; in the derivative Torah tradition, it is the naming and protecting of widows, orphans, and immigrants, the very ones the empire characteristically finds expendable.
- In turn Jesus touched all kinds of outsiders who were undocumented nobodies in the empire. In his Terry Lectures, Terry Eagleton has championed this particularizing narrative of the neighborhood against the neoatheists who are themselves ensconced in the Enlightenment narrative of empire. Eagleton, however, does not make a cognitive argument about ontological matters as is the way in which the neoatheists have framed the question. Instead he makes a moral-neighborly argument by observing the way in which Jesus comes "from below" to stand in solidarity with "the scum of the earth." He observes that Jesus fits none of the expectations of empire:

> Jesus, unlike most responsible American citizens, appears to do no work, and is accused of being a glutton and a drunk-

ard. He is presented as homeless, propertyless, celibate, peripatetic, socially marginal, disdainful of kinsfolk, without a trade, a friend of outcasts and pariahs, averse to material possessions, without fear for his own safety, careless about purity regulations, critical of traditional authority, a thorn in the side of the Establishment, and a scourge of the rich and powerful.[17]

He authorized and enacted a morality that in effect subverts the claims and practices of the empire:

The morality Jesus preaches is reckless, extravagant, improvident, over-the-top, a scandal to actuaries and a stumbling block to real estate agents: forgive your enemies, give away your cloak as well as your coat, turn the other cheek, love those who insult you, walk the extra mile, take no thought for tomorrow.[18]

He champions those who live in chronic transgression:

To the outrage of the Zealots, Pharisees, and right-wing rednecks of all ages, this body is dedicated in particular to all those losers, deadbeats, riffraff, and colonial collaborators who are not righteous but flamboyantly unrighteous — who either live in chronic transgression of the Mosaic law or, like the Gentiles, fall outside its sway altogether.[19]

He evokes a new community that contradicts the empire and breaks the totalism in every dimension:

17. Terry Eagleton, *Reason, Faith, and Revolution: Reflections on the God Debate* (New Haven: Yale University Press, 2009), 10.
18. Eagleton, *Reason, Faith, and Revolution*, 14.
19. Eagleton, *Reason, Faith, and Revolution*, 20.

The only authentic image of this violently loving God is a tortured and executed political criminal, who dies in an act of solidarity with what the Bible calls the *anawim*, meaning the destitute and dispossessed. Crucifixion was reserved by the Romans for political offenses alone. The *anawim*, in Pauline phrase, are the shit of the earth — the scum and refuse of society who constitute the cornerstone of the new form of human life known as the kingdom of God. Jesus himself is consistently presented as their representative.[20]

His transformative action pivots on attentiveness to the disqualified:

The blind receive their sight, the lame walk, the lepers are cleansed, the deaf hear, the dead are raised, the poor have good news brought to them. (Luke 7:22)

It is precisely from this practice of empowerment of the disqualified that evokes a different kind of community that the Pauline trajectory can identify an alternative network of conduct which he terms "the fruits of the Spirit." These "fruits" contradict the empire with its "works of the flesh." Kahl concludes:

It is against this false law observance, which is driven by "fleshly" needs of public conformity *(euprosōpēsai),* this obscuring the proper obedience of law as Torah, that Paul puts up the "law of Christ" as the law of the crucified *one* who is *other* ([Galatians] 6:2, 14). It builds community not through trying to gain advantage over one another, but through "bearing one another's burdens" (6:2). What counts is nei-

20. Eagleton, *Reason, Faith, and Revolution,* 23.

ther circumcision nor foreskin, nor any other of the publicly recognized status markers of distinction, honor, and shame, but rather "faith working through love" (5:6) as the works of peace that signal a new creation (6:14-15). Apart from the works of imperial law, these faith works of love for Paul are indispensable, an insight that has been obscured by the abstract Protestant antithesis of faith versus works. Love of "your neighbor as your self" as the complete fulfillment of Torah (5:14) and the "new" law of Christ (5:6; 6:2) does not abandon Jewish law as such but rather the competitive and combative hierarchy of self and other that is at the core of Roman imperial *nomos*.[21]

The lists of such "fruits" are well known to us, but they have not usually been understood in systemic fashion with reference to the empire. In Galatians, the catalogue counters the "combat order" with neighborly attentiveness:

> By contrast, the fruit of the Spirit is love, joy, peace, patience, kindness, generosity, faithfulness, gentleness, and self-control. There is no law against such things. (5:22-23)

In the derivative trajectory, the lists vary but each time include "forgiveness," a stance unknown and unacceptable to empire:

> Be kind to one another, tenderhearted, forgiving one another, as God in Christ has forgiven you. (Ephesians 4:32)

---

21. Kahl, *Galatians Re-Imagined*, 270-72. Philip Carrington, *The Primitive Christian Catechism: A Study in the Epistles* (Cambridge: Cambridge University Press, 1940), has persuasively argued that these catalogues are part of a recurring sequence that reflects the processes of baptism. Thus the baptized come under the discipline of these lists of "fruits of the spirit" in renunciation of the "works of the flesh."

As God's chosen ones, holy and beloved, clothe yourselves with compassion, kindness, humility, meekness, and patience. Bear with one another and, if anyone has a complaint against another, forgive each other; just as the Lord has forgiven you, so you also must forgive. Above all, clothe yourselves with love, which binds everything together in perfect harmony. (Colossians 3:12-14)

We are bound to acknowledge, in expositing this alternative narrative, that it, like the imperial narrative, is not an ontological given. The baptismal narrative that evokes and legitimates neighborly community is also a social construction, a proposal, an advocacy, a possibility that depends upon and assures the conviction that the narrative of empire has no prior claim upon us. Thus this alternative narrative joins issue with the imperial narrative. It is not an even contest or a level playing field. The imperial narrative has many advantages at the outset, not least that we are all to some extent in thrall to that narrative. But the issue is joined!

III.

It is my judgment, then, that contestation on behalf of this alternative narrative is the deep work of the parish and the deep claim of the church. That contestation, moreover, is most acutely urgent in our society, given the nearly unchecked and immediate force of the narrative of empire among us. Indeed, the more the practical inadequacy of that narrative becomes evident because it cannot make us safe and cannot make us happy, the more vigorously it is championed in a way that is remote from the lived facts on the ground.

I take it that it is this uneven contestation that makes pastoral ministry and parish life so difficult in our particular social circumstance. The church and its pastors have the task of making the case for this narrative of neighborly particularity by talk and by walk, by face-to-face *generosity*, by daily *hospitality*, and by incredible *forgiveness*. Such a way is in defiance of the imperial narrative that is *parsimonious* for those not at the top of the pyramid, that is *inhospitable* to those who are not achievers and performers in service of empire, and that is impatiently *unforgiving* of those who do not measure up to the requirements of empire.

It is clear that by talk and by walk, the church, even in its conventional life, is committed to the practice of this counternarrative. But what is not often undertaken is a parallel task that I take to be crucial, namely, the exposé of the narrative of empire as inadequate, surely false, and ultimately lethal. It is, in my judgment, as necessary as it is hazardous to expose the imperial narrative as inadequate, for until it is recognized as such, a decision for an alternative is very difficult. The imperial narrative in American lore, moreover, continues to seduce us into imagining that we can "win" and succeed in the rat race that is indispensable for the empire. The continuing powerful notion of exceptionalism that powers imperial imagination is based, I believe, on three uncritical assumptions:

1. Enlightenment rationality takes technical knowledge as power in the service of control without any critical limit. So totalizing is this claim that every facet of "people knowledge" is made to seem foolish and unimpressive.
2. Market ideology specializes in competitive individualism in the service of self-sufficiency. Exposé of this ideology requires class analysis that permits us to see that "the market" is not at all even-handed, but works to the advantage of the already advantaged and to the disadvantage of the already disadvantaged. But of course calling attention to such disproportion is immediately labeled as "class warfare" by those

who want to keep advantage hidden under the guise of the neutrality of the market.

3. U.S. exceptionalism adds a veneer of legitimacy to the claims of rationality and market ideology, a moral sense of entitlement that keeps many have-nots mesmerized by the claims of entitlement to that to which they will never have access.

That combination of Enlightenment rationality, market ideology, and political exceptionalism with its tinge of evangelical approval is the "Authorized Version" of common life in our society. It becomes the norm for the management of money and power. In the face of that, the gospel tradition, rooted in ancient Israel, pivoting on Jesus, and entrusted to the church, is at best a *sub*-version of reality that functions to *sub*-vert the Authorized Version. But of course, the subverting of Authorized Reality is open to many tellings in many subversions, so that there rises up in Christian parlance a "Revised Standard Version" and a "New Revised Standard Version" of reality, always again a subversion that arises in the particularity of practice. Indeed,

every time the book is opened,
every time the bread is broken,
every time the cup is poured out,
every time the towel is wrapped around the feet of a beggar,

the subversion does its work and receives fresh formulation. The narrative of the neighborhood does not trade in large absolute edicts. It proceeds always in sacramental gestures, calling attention to the truth that is bodily and transformable, the very truth the empire does not notice and cannot credit. That is why we dare to say,

We all share the Word, one bread, one cup.

When we derive our vocabulary from the Scriptures, from the loaf and the cup, we find ourselves entrusted with a way of talk about brother and sister and sacrament and hope and obedience and resistance — all terms that make no sense in the empire, for such claims cannot be accommodated to the goals of empire.

My exposition of these two narratives leads me to awarenesses that are important to my own faith:

1. For a very long time we followers of Jesus have settled for the narrative of empire as the framing truth of our common life, and we have settled for the narrative of the neighborhood in private and in intimate particularity.

2. Jesus declared to his disciples that we cannot have it both ways — not "God and mammon," not empire and neighborhood (Matthew 6:24). In the next verse, he invited his disciples not to be anxious, for he understood, surely, that it is seeking to have it both ways that is the ground of devouring anxiety.

3. We live in a context where advocacy for the neighborhood is not only urgent, but I think now welcome. It is welcome, in my judgment, because many people are now able to see that the narrative of empire has failed. Many people know down deep that Enlightenment rationality, valuable as it is, does not give access to the truth that we must have to live. Many people know down deep that market ideology is in fact a recipe for predation. Many people know down deep that U.S. exceptionalism is not sustainable in the world we face. For quite a long while we have been mindful of that unsustainability, but now, especially since September 11, 2001, that reality has become unavoidably palpable. As a consequence, many people are wondering about an alternative account of reality whereby society (and its economy) can be organized differently.

I believe it is an open question about how seriously we in the church, especially we pastors, want to press the point. I know how difficult that is and how ambivalent we ourselves are. And surely I do not have in mind any confrontational posture with this issue. Robert Jenson has stated the matter in a most frontal way that invites close study and reflection:

> We must summon the audacity to say that modernity's scientific/metaphysical metanarrative — at the moment told by astrophysicists and neo-Darwinians — is not the encompassing story within which all other accounts of reality must establish their places, or be discredited by failing to find one. It is instead a rather brutal abstraction from reality. The abstraction has proved to be magnificent in its intellectual power and practical benefits. Nevertheless, by these disciplines' methodological eschewal of teleology, they prevent themselves from describing what actually is. As pop scientists urge over and over, the tale told by Scripture and creed finds no comfortable place within modernity's metanarrative. It is time for the church simply to reply: this is certainly the case, and the reason it is the case is that the tale told by Scripture is too comprehensive to find place within so drastically curtailed a version of the facts. Indeed, the gospel story cannot fit within *any* other would-be metanarrative because it is itself the only true metanarrative — or it is altogether false.[22]

The joining of the issue in this way clarifies. It is easy enough, from the perspective of Enlightenment rationality (and its companions, market ideology and exceptionalism), to judge that the church's narrative of neighborhood authorized by God is a "fairy

---

22. Robert W. Jenson, *Canon and Creed* (Louisville: Westminster John Knox, 2010), 120.

tale." But what if the reverse turns out to be the case? What if, from the perspective of the neighborhood, the imperial exposition of Enlightenment reason, market ideology, and political exceptionalism is the real fairy tale, a tale told to protect hidden advantage so that the narrative covers over social reality with all of its truth and all of its potential?

As concerns the practice of the church, I believe:

1. That the health of the pastor depends on clarity about the narrative that yields our defining baptismal identity;
2. That we are immobilized and at risk by our own ambivalence about these narratives;
3. That the fidelity (and therefore the survival) of the church depends on not having it both ways, but in our being clear and straightforward in order that we may challenge the unexamined ontological assumptions concerning the priority of the imperial narrative. Thus for all of our anxiety about the survival of the church, the real issue is not whether an institution with order, program, budget, and glorious heritage can survive. What matters, I suggest, is whether there will be a sustainable force for this witness in a world that is organized against such a witness of Friday and Sunday.

The first time I presented these thoughts, I did so to the clergy of the Episcopal Diocese of Southern Ohio on February 7, 2012. As it happened, that day, so Bishop Breidenthal told me, was the saint day of the Roman centurion at the foot of the cross in the gospel of Matthew. You will recall that as the curtain of the temple was torn and the centurion observed the earthquake that ensued on that Friday, he was moved to a staggering awareness that Matthew narrates in this way:

Truly this man was God's Son. (Matthew 27:54)

That awesome moment of awareness on the part of the armed agent to the empire is the narrative acknowledgement a) that the narrative of Jesus as Son of God is true and b) that the narrative of Caesar to whom the centurion had owed allegiance is, perforce, false. That acknowledgement is an epitome of the drama of "switching narratives," the drama that is the primary public work of the church.[23] Indeed, as the apostles discovered in the book of Acts, there is no more compelling or dangerous action than to blurt out, "Christ is risen!" Nor is there any more dangerous complexity for the congregation than the response, "He is risen indeed!"

The pastoral task, I judge, is now to conduct that contestation (which the centurion has modeled) among folk who are deeply ambivalent about participating in the contest. The reason it is such a hard time in the church (and potentially such a great time for the church) is that our unrecognized collusion with the imperial narrative and the hidden contradictions between the narratives are now increasingly exposed. That exposé now requires of us choices that we have not had to make in any recent time, decisions that we do not want to make. We are deciding about the truth and the fairy tale. We have been brought to this place by God where we stand alongside the Roman governor with his anguished wonderment, "What is truth?" (John 18:38).[24] We know the answer to that question, wondrous and dangerous as it is to utter it.

23. On the process of "switching stories," see Peter L. Berger and Thomas Luckmann, *The Social Construction of Reality: A Treatise in the Sociology of Knowledge* (Garden City: Doubleday, 1966), 156-57.

24. See the compelling exposition of the trial by Paul Lehmann, *The Transfiguration of Politics: The Presence and Power of Jesus of Nazareth in and over Human Affairs* (New York: Harper & Row, 1975), 48-70.

V I

Concluding Summation

The believer possesses the eternally certain antidote to despair, viz., possibility; for with God all things are possible every instant. This is the sound health of faith which resolves contradictions. . . . The fatalist is in despair — he has lost God, and therefore himself as well; for if he has no God, neither has he a self. . . . Inasmuch as for God all things are possible, it may be said that this is what God is, viz., one for whom all things are possible.

SØREN KIERKEGAARD

My argument in the foregoing concerning "three urgent prophetic tasks" depends upon two interpretive maneuvers that merit comment. First, the sequence of *ideology-denial-despair* and the counterpoint of *realism-grief-hope* may strike one as much too schematic. I do not intend it as a rigid scheme, but only as a general guide for the way in which human persons and human communities move through the process of loss and recovery. Such a pattern is confirmed by what we know about "grief work" as offered by Granger Westberg, long before the more noticed work of Elisabeth Kübler-Ross.[1] More

1. Granger E. Westberg, *Good Grief: A Faith-Based Guide to Understanding and Healing* (Minneapolis: Augsburg Fortress, 1997).

important for my argument than contemporary understandings of loss and grief, however, is the recognition that the movement I have traced follows the sequence of ancient Israel in its deep faith crisis concerning the loss of Jerusalem. Most clearly, this sequence I have suggested is voiced in the sequence of biblical literature of Jeremiah-Lamentations-2 Isaiah, though it is not confined to those elements of the tradition:

- Jeremiah is the great voice of realism against the ideology of Jerusalem.
- Lamentations is the most compelling performance of grief that precludes denial in that ancient tradition.
- 2 Isaiah is the best known and most eloquent voice of hope in ancient Israel that counters despair.

Thus the sequence I have outlined remains very close to the sequence in the life of Israel reflected in the Old Testament itself. Readers who know my work will see, as well, a close parallel to my interpretations of the Psalms as a sequence of orientation/disorientation/new orientation.[2] Thus,

- ideology reflects the *old orientation* that must be broken by realism;
- denial gives way to grief as *disorientation* is acknowledged;
- *new orientation* becomes possible as hope overrides despair.

In both prophetic and Psalms traditions the sequence can be traced. In the prophets the pivot point is the destruction of Jerusalem. In the Psalms the poetry may turn around any number of experienced crises. In the laments over Jerusalem (as in Psalms

2. Walter Brueggemann, *The Psalms and the Life of Faith*, ed. Patrick D. Miller (Minneapolis: Fortress, 1995), 3-32.

74 and 79), the focus is unmistakably on the crisis of Jerusalem, as it is in the prophetic traditions.

The second interpretive maneuver I have made is to proceed on the assumption that the emergency of 9/11 is, for U.S. society, a compelling analogy to the emergency of ancient Jerusalem. James A. Sanders has used the phrase "dynamic analogy" to characterize the way in which the Old Testament continues to "reperform" old memories in new circumstances.[3] The clearest case in the Old Testament for such practice is the way in which the Exodus memory is reperformed in the Isaiah tradition concerning the return from Babylonian exile (Isaiah 40:3-5; 41:17-20; 42:14-16; 43:1-3, 14-21).[4] The analogy is obviously imperfect; that is, I take it, what Sanders means by "dynamic" in his phrase. The analogy is suggestive and elusive and not fixed or stable. In the same way, I suggest that the analogy for the destruction of ancient Jerusalem in 9/11 is imperfect at best. But I find, nevertheless, that the analogy works, because in the latter case as in the former, the crisis is that the destruction attests the failure of the ideological claim of invulnerability grounded in exceptionalism. Thus I have suggested that 9/11 is a symbol and an epitome of the wide and deep loss now faced in our society that requires rethinking from the ground up.

Beyond that analogy, then, I suggest that the political economy of the United States, emboldened by liturgical reinforcement, now requires rethinking in a most imaginative way. Such rethinking is indeed the work of prophetic imagination that has a calling, I do not doubt, to walk our society into the crisis where it does not want

3. James A. Sanders, *Canon and Community: A Guide to Canonical Criticism* (Guides to Biblical Scholarship; Philadelphia: Fortress, 1984), 44.

4. See Bernhard W. Anderson, "Exodus Typology in Second Isaiah," in *Israel's Prophetic Heritage: Essays in Honor of James Muilenburg*, ed. Anderson and Walter Harrelson (New York: Harper, 1962), 177-95; "Exodus and Covenant in Second Isaiah and Prophetic Tradition," in *Magnalia Dei: The Mighty Acts of God; Essays on the Bible and Archaeology in Memory of G. Ernest Wright*, ed. Frank Moore Cross, Werner E. Lemke, and Patrick D. Miller, Jr. (Garden City: Doubleday, 1976), 339-60.

to go, and to walk our society out of that crisis into newness that it does not believe is possible. That walk into and walk out of, in quite terse expression, is exactly the assignment given to Jeremiah:

> See, today I appoint you over nations and over kingdoms,
> to pluck up and to pull down,
> to destroy and to overthrow,
> to build and to plant. (Jeremiah 1:10)

That twofold ministry is possible when the ideology is broken and the community begins to deal with the world that is in front of us.

The establishment sequence of ideology-denial-despair is the predictable work of dominant culture. That culture believes that everything has a technical solution that depends primarily on money, power, and know-how. If that culture has enough money to pay for its preferences, enough power to work its will, and enough know-how to work a fix in technical form, it can accomplish, so it believes, self-security.

But of course the prophetic tradition — rooted in the old covenant — knows that the defining requirements of a society are not technical and do not admit of technical resolution. Because the covenantal-prophetic tradition is grounded in relational reality, it knows that what is required for the happiness and safety of the body politic is what is required in the old covenantal habits of justice, righteousness, and steadfast love.

Thus I propose that the oracular dictum of Jeremiah offers a faithful rendition of the map of choices that are always before the human community and that are now before our political economy in our moment of post-9/11 crisis:

> Thus says the LORD: Do not let the wise boast in their wisdom, do not let the mighty boast in their might, do not let the wealthy boast in their wealth; but let those who boast

boast in this, that they understand and know me, that I am
the LORD; I act with steadfast love, justice, and righteousness in the earth, for in these things I delight, says the LORD.
(Jeremiah 9:23-24)

Prophetic rhetoric, faithful to the claims of covenant, states the
matter in a deep and nonnegotiable either/or:

Either ideology or realism;
Either denial or grief;
Either despair or hope.

That deep either/or is as old as the covenant:

See, I have set before you today life and prosperity, death and
adversity. If you obey the commandments of the Lord your
God that I am commanding you today, by loving the LORD your
God, walking in his ways, and observing his commandments,
decrees, and ordinances, then you shall live and become numerous, and the LORD your God will bless you in the land that
you are entering to possess. But if your heart turns away and
you do not hear, but are led astray to bow down to other gods
and serve them, I declare to you today that you shall perish;
you shall not live long in the land that you are crossing the
Jordan to enter and possess. (Deuteronomy 30:15-18)

It is as urgent as the summons of Joshua:

Now if you are unwilling to serve the LORD, choose this day
whom you will serve . . . but as for me and my household, we
will serve the LORD. (Joshua 24:15)

It is as risky as the contest at Mount Carmel:

How long will you go limping with two different opinions?
If the LORD is God, follow him; but if Baal, then follow him.
(1 Kings 18:21)

It is as singular as in the summons of Jesus:

Enter through the narrow gate; for the gate is wide and the
road is easy that leads to destruction, and there are many
who take it. For the gate is narrow and the road is hard that
leads to life, and there are few who find it. (Matthew 7:13-14)

This either/or of two alternative ways of life is congruent with
what we know about the psychological processes of grief and loss,
and what we know sociologically about the human infrastructure
that is indispensable for a viable human community. In the end,
however, the matter is a theological one that concerns what kind
of will and purpose governs the life of the world. The final phrase
of the Jeremiah oracle has YHWH say:

In these things I delight. (Jeremiah 9:24)

This rhetoric is a prophetic way to say that at bottom the Holy
Agent who orders the world is deeply committed to a relational
reality. YHWH, the creator of heaven and earth, has shaped the
world for relationships. That is why I have begun this discussion
with "the neighborhood." And no amount of imperial finesse — of
money, power, or know-how — can finally overcome the resilient
gift and requirement of neighborly relatedness.[5]

In the end, my exposition is an effort at quite practical theology concerning the life of the church. When it is faithful, the

---

5. It will be readily recognized that Martin Buber, *I and Thou* (New York:
Scribner's, 1937), has offered the most elemental version of this contrast.

church — the local congregation as the defining unit of faith — is committed to an alternative neighborly practice of the world. It does so in the face of shrill, insistent reductionism that wants to eliminate the inconvenience of neighborly obligations.

Thus it is the church that *practices realism* in the face of ideology vouching for "God and country" and all that the mantra signifies. The realism of the church is grounded in nothing less than the "embodiment" of the life-giving God in Jesus Christ and in the derivative practice of the Eucharist, whereby we refuse the denial of the bodily world that lives by bread. That festival of bread named "Gratitude" calls the church always again to attend to the bodily historical reality of the neighbors, concerning hunger, poverty, and all the other "diseases of Egypt" that serve the pyramidic accumulation of power and money at the expense of the neighbor (Exodus 15:26; Deuteronomy 7:15; 28:60). It is the church that keeps the bodily reality of the world in purview and refuses the cover-ups of the empire.

Thus it is the church that *practices and performs grief* while the world conventionally denies the power of death among us. It is the church — after the manner of covenantal Israel — that has practiced the honesty of mourning that is essential for continuing to live freely in a world of profound loss.

Thus it is the church that *performs hope* in a world of despair. The church regularly performs the rhetoric and gestures of forgiveness with the prospect of beginning again in newness.

For the sake of your Son Jesus Christ,
have mercy on us and forgive us;
that we may delight in your will,
and walk in your ways,
to the glory of your Name. Amen.[6]

6. *The Book of Common Prayer* (New York: Seabury, 1979), 352.

The church moreover reiterates its central affirmation of new possibility after the momentary victory of death:

Christ is risen!
He is risen indeed!

We may and do quibble about many matters in the church. But however we may parse those quibbles, we share this confession of newness, given in ways we know not how, at the bottomless pit of death. And we begin again!

Thus the prophetic tasks of realism, grief, and hope are not odd interpretations or incidental add-ons to the life of the church. They are, rather, the most elemental truth that belongs to the identity and life of the church. These acts of realism, grief, and hope are everywhere present in the life, the talk, and walk of the church. What the church does not do so well, I think, is to join issue in named ways with the narrative of death that is performed by the empire. We continue to imagine, much of the time, that somehow the narrative of neighborliness (realism, grief, hope) and narrative of empire (ideology, denial, despair) can be at peace with each other.[7]

But of course they cannot. So Jesus could instruct his disciples:

No one can serve two masters; for a slave will either hate the one and love the other, or be devoted to the one and despise the other. You cannot serve God and wealth. (Matthew 6:24)

Ours is a time, I propose, when this issue will inescapably have

---

7. The clearest, most dramatic case of this in recent time is the "German Christians" in Hitler's Germany who imagined that they could have it both ways with the Gospel and with National Socialism. Indeed, the familiar phrase "cheap grace" arose amid crisis, the assumption that one does not need to choose between two deep claims.

to be joined. It is best that we do it knowingly. To be knowing is to recognize that the Gospel embodied in Jesus of Nazareth is one definitive reach of the best faith of ancient Israel. Thus there is a direct line from the dictum of Jeremiah to the lyric of Paul:

> Do not let the wise boast in their wisdom, do not let the mighty boast in their might, do not let the wealthy boast in their wealth; but let those who boast boast in this, that they understand and know me, that I am the LORD; I act with steadfast love, justice, and righteousness in the earth, for in these things I delight, says the LORD. (Jeremiah 9:23-24)

> For God's foolishness is wiser than human wisdom, and God's weakness is stronger than human strength . . . to reduce to nothing things that are . . . as it is written, "Let the one who boasts, boast in the Lord." (1 Corinthians 1:25-31)

In the end Paul aligns his affirmation with that of Jeremiah. Prophetic work is to be faithful in boasting of the right things!

.